Twayne's English Authors Series

Sylvia E. Bowman, *General Editor*

INDIANA UNIVERSITY

Thomas Dekker

(TEAS) 71

Thomas Dekker

By GEORGE R. PRICE

Michigan State University

Twayne Publishers, Inc.　: :　New York

FOR I. G. P.

Preface

No Elizabethan writer except Shakespeare, Jonson, and Marlowe has benefited more from the attention of scholars of the first rank during the last half century than has Thomas Dekker. Probably the two major contributions are Professor Fredson Bowers's excellent critical edition of the plays and Mme. M. T. Jones-Davies's encyclopedic study of Dekker's work, both dramatic and non-dramatic, in relation to Elizabethan life and culture. Both of these masterpieces have appeared within the last ten years. Particularly in view of Mme. Jones-Davies's exhaustive work, a word of explanation may be needed for the existence of this book.

Although Dekker's importance in Renaissance literature is sufficient reason for more reappraisals of him than have been made, the primary justification for this book lies in the multiple audiences for which Twayne's English Authors Series is intended. *Un peintre de la vie londonienne: Thomas Dekker* (Paris, 1958) is addressed, I believe, first of all to French scholars and literati; for without question, if it were designed for British and American students and scholars, it would need to be compressed. As used by Elizabethan specialists, it is likely to be chiefly a work of reference to be consulted on particular topics. Because the work is written in French, it will be difficult for some American students and lay readers to use, especially those who wish to make a rapid survey of Dekker's achievement. Hence, there seems to be a place for a book less exhaustive than Mme. Jones-Davies's.

I had composed this book before I read *Un peintre*. On reading it, I have not only been struck with admiration for Mme. Jones-Davies's scholarship, but also pleased to find how often our opinions agree. There are, of course, occasional differences of interpretation or inference; but I have decided to leave my statements unqualified by reference to her views because, in so short a study as this which deals with a large body of writings, there is no room for argument. However, I have adopted her opinion about two minor works which I had overlooked and have inserted those two items in the "Selected Bibliography." I may add that the close parallelism between Mme. Jones-Davies's chronological canon of Dekker's works and my own, prepared thus independently, has been especially pleasing to me and perhaps will also reassure the reader. I excluded from my list, however, a few works which appear in hers simply because it is the plan of Mme. Jones-Davies (but not mine) to include the title of any work which has been connected in some way with Dekker, no matter how doubtfully.

Claiming no high originality for my point of view, I wish to point out that my approach, particularly to the plays, has been an attempt to discover as fully as possible how Dekker utilized early Elizabethan dramatic traditions. If I have succeeded well in this effort, the book will have been justified. To illustrate Dekker's range of themes and degrees of seriousness, as well as the influence of contemporary dramatic vogues upon him, I have chosen eight plays whose dates range from 1599 to 1623. They include *Old Fortunatus, The Shoemaker's Holiday, Satiromastix,* Parts I and II of *The Honest Whore, The Whore of Babylon, If This Be Not a Good Play, the Devil Is in It,* and *Match Me in London.* The terms *moral fantasy, romance, personal satire, realism, patriotic allegory, social satire,* and *tragicomic intrigue* may describe the modes of these plays.

Criticism of Dekker's dramatic work is complicated by the fact that, except for John Fletcher, he was the most facile and frequent collaborator in the Elizabethan age. Indeed, a few of Dekker's collaborations have enjoyed almost as much critical esteem as the best of his independent plays. I have given an account of four of the collaborations (in addition to Part I of *The Honest Whore*): *Patient Grissil, The Virgin Martyr, The Witch of Edmonton,* and *The Sun's Darling.* Respectively, these are specimens of moral *exemplum,* Jacobean rendering of a saint's legend, domestic tragedy, and another moral fantasy. Except for the history play and Fletcherian tragedy, I have omitted no genre that Dekker wrote. Of his histories the only survivor is the

mutilated play, *Sir Thomas Wyatt;* of Fletcherian tragedy, the
only example is *The Noble Spanish Soldier.*

The chief critical material of the remainder of the book is an
account of Dekker's non-dramatic work, both prose and verse,
and an analysis of his religious and social principles. I have tried
to relate the prose, in particular, to the popular literature of
that age; but for both prose and verse, I have tried to make an
essentially literary, rather than just a historical, judgment of the
works analyzed. Because of Dekker's assumed function of re-
former in his non-dramatic pieces, an outline of his religious and
social ideas is pertinent. Finally, in one section of the Bibliography ("Primary Sources"), I have listed all of Dekker's works in
chronological order. Aside from Mme. Jones-Davies's similar
bibliography in *Un peintre,* this is the first attempt in many
years to establish the Dekker canon in the order of composition.

The availability of Professor Bowers's edition of the plays and
of F. P. Wilson's of the plague pamphlets has made accurate
quotation easy from those major sources. I trust that retention of
their somewhat modified old-spelling texts will not frustrate readers unaccustomed to using Elizabethan books in their original
form. Generally, I have followed Professor Bowers's practice of
rendering literary titles in modern spelling; the wide use of a
few Elizabethan titles in their original spelling, however, has led
me into inconsistency in this respect. All citations of passages
in the plays, then, are to be understood as taken from *The Dramatic Works of Thomas Dekker,* edited by Fredson Bowers (Cambridge, 1953–1961); passages in the non-dramatic works are
from *The Plague Pamphlets of Thomas Dekker,* edited by
F. P. Wilson (Oxford, 1925), and (other than those tracts) from
The Non-Dramatic Works of Thomas Dekker, edited by Alexander B. Grosart (London, 1884–1885). Other editions that I
have used are cited specifically in the footnotes.

I wish to acknowledge gratefully my obligation to the Depart-
ment of English of Michigan State University for granting me a
term's leave for the advancement of this work. I thank also Miss
Sylvia Bowman, General Editor, for her understanding treatment, and my wife for her helpful criticism of my manuscript.

Michigan State University

G.R.P.

Contents

Chronology

Besides the references to Thomas Dekker in Philip Henslowe's record of theater finance, which is discussed in Chapter 1, research by F. P. Wilson and Professor Mark Eccles has provided the most significant biographical data we possess.[1] Professor G. E. Bentley's account in *The Jacobean and Caroline Stage*, III (Oxford, 1956), 241–245, incorporates their findings as well as some of Mary L. Hunt's inferences in *Thomas Dekker* (New York, 1911). A. H. Bullen's article in *The Dictionary of National Biography* needs correction at a number of points.

Because of the special problems of ascription in the work of an Elizabethan playwright and pamphleteer, problems which inevitably demand at least a brief comment on many items, it seems necessary to separate the mere biographical data from the chronicle of Dekker's authorship. Hence, the few biographical facts and inferences are given below; Dekker's works are arranged in time-order in the Bibliography under "Primary Sources." The index of this book locates items in the Bibliography as well as in the text.

1572? Thomas Dekker born in London of unknown parentage.

1580?–1588? Presumably attends grammar school.

1589–1593? Probably serves as a seaman or as an apprentice to a tradesman.

1592?–1593? Marriage.

1594 A child of "Thomas Dycker" is baptized in St. Giles, Cripplegate.

1593?–1595? Probably begins to write for the actors, particularly Henslowe's clients, the Lord Admiral's Men.

1598 Henslowe first mentions Dekker by name in January. Francis Meres lists Dekker among the best English writers of tragedy. Early in February, Dekker is in prison for debt.

1599 Arrested on January 30, for debt to the Lord Chamberlain's Men; Henslowe discharges debt.

1600–1601 Writes for the Children of Paul's company; drawn into the Stage Quarrel against Jonson. Writes occasionally for Henslowe, that is, for the Lord Admiral's Men.

1602 Writes on full-time basis for Henslowe.

1603 Composes much of the script for *The Magnificent Entertainment Given to King James.*

1603–1604 Composes two pamphlets on the cause and the misery of plague.

1604 Resumes playwriting for Henslowe, the Children of Paul's, and probably also the Prince's Men. Collaborates with Middleton (at least two plays) and with Webster (two), 1604–1606.

1606–circa 1609 Quarrel with the Prince's Men at the Fortune Theater; Children of Paul's company collapses. Dekker writes prose tracts.

1610–1612 Returns to playwriting, apparently for the Queen's Men at the Red Bull Theater; continues to write tracts and at least one Lord Mayor's show. Moves from Cripplegate to Clerkenwell, near the Red Bull.

1613–1619 Confined in King's Bench prison for debt.

1616 Wife, Mary, buried from St. James's, Clerkenwell.

1620–1624 Writes for the Red Bull Company (now called "Players of the Revels"), for the Palsgrave's Men, and possibly for others. Collaborates with Massinger, Day, Ford, Webster, and others.

1625 Death of King James; plague causes closing of the theaters, reorganization of the acting companies. Publishes tract.

1626–1629 Indicted for recusancy, probably because of absence from church to avoid arrest for debt. Composes three tracts; writes at least two Lord Mayor's shows; revises or composes several plays.

1630 Resurgence of the plague leads Dekker to publish two more pamphlets.

1631 Probably returns to playwriting; assignment of plays to this year is conjectural.

1632 Buried on August 25 from St. James's parish, Clerkenwell.

Thomas Dekker

CHAPTER 1

Dekker's Life (1572?-1632)

SEVERAL times Thomas Dekker remarked that he had been born and reared in London; he was less definite about the year of his birth, but we have good reason to think that it was 1572.[1] As yet, no documents have been discovered that tell unquestionably of what parentage or in which parish he was born. The playwright consistently spelled his name, unquestionably Dutch, as we do now; other spellings on title pages of works of which he was wholly or partly the author are always accompanied by bibliographical evidence that a scribe or typesetter composed the title page. In accord with the literary conventions of his time, Dekker gives no autobiographical sketch or references in his tracts. He shows a knowledge of the Dutch language that is quite unusual among the dramatists; however, the spirit of his references to the Dutch people and their customs is always jocular and often contemptuous. A reasonable inference may be that his progenitors were Dutch immigrants, but not his own parents. Dekker regards himself as English through and through.

In 1615, Edward Howes, in continuing Stowe's *Annales*, lists Dekker—then about forty-three and in debtors' prison—as among the poets of England and entitles him a "gentleman."[2] We should not take the "gentleman" to indicate Howe's knowledge of Dekker's gentle birth, for the annalist also assigns the term to Christopher Marlowe, Ben Jonson, Thomas Heywood, and others, thereby dignifying a cobbler's son, a former bricklayer, and an actor. More significantly, Howes thus testifies to the fact that, by the seventeenth century, a man of any origin might be considered a gentleman if he possessed a respectable knowledge of Latin poetry and was also a professional man of letters.

I *Education*

Since no records of Dekker's education have been discovered, we can only make inferences about it from the learning he reveals in his plays and tracts, as well as from his milieu in general. Therefore, we suppose that, as a little boy, Dekker was sent to a dame school to learn the elements of religion, reading, writing, and arithmetic. At about seven, he probably entered a grammar school in London or a nearby town. It should be noted, however, that Dekker's writings reveal no intimate knowledge of natural creatures or country life; his references to such things are in the general language of a man reared in the city, in contrast to Shakespeare's closer observation of "wrens with little quills" and "sunburnt sicklemen of August weary." This negative evidence suggests that Dekker's grammar school was in London, not (like John Keats's) in a nearby small town.

No record exists of Dekker's attending a university. His few references to Oxford and Cambridge are most casual and reveal neither the knowledge nor spirit of an alumnus—a significant point when we observe that one of Dekker's commonest themes for indignation is society's neglect of scholars. Consequently, to estimate the extent of his schooling we must judge by the reading he evidences in his works. Dekker's quotations from Latin poets are impressively numerous and show, I believe, the range of reading that a good grammar-school education could provide or at least provoke.[3] We may suppose, then, that, like young Ben Jonson, Dekker was a bookish boy, an apt pupil of a master who readily imparted his love of literature.

Yet, whoever the master was, the mind he helped to form did not imbibe the spirit of Augustan literature to the degree that Jonson's did. There is a little innocent vainglory in Dekker's display of Latin. More important, it must be admitted that, unlike Jonson, Dekker, as a man of letters, does not strive for strict unity of theme; and he labors less over "well-turned and true-filed lines" in either plays or tracts. On the other hand, Dekker's delight in the melody and sentiment of Ovid and Virgil did not preclude a relish for the wit of Martial and Horace. However, though Dekker at times attempts the role of satirist, the impulse appears to come from sources other than the Classics.

II   *The Milieu*

The Elizabethan London in which the schoolboy Dekker grew up is, of course, reflected in many of his writings. But as a basis for better understanding of the author, we should glance, most superficially, at his milieu. In 1572, the year of Dekker's birth, London with its suburbs made a city of about a hundred thousand people. It was, and it remained for generations, a crowded place; for it received annually an influx of Englishmen dispossessed of their homes in the shires or unable to make a living there, as well as great numbers of Huguenots, Flemings, and Dutchmen who came as refugees from war or persecution. No adequate provisions for renovation or for new building were enforced in London during Dekker's lifetime. As a result, some sections were heavily overpopulated. Probably the worst slum conditions, however, were those in the suburban areas which grew up along the high roads and were subjected to little control from the county government. These, such as Shoreditch and Southwark, were the special haunts of poverty, vice, and crime.

On the other hand, young Dekker saw many picturesque streets and fine buildings within the city proper. Often he had been told of the lightning and fire which, in 1561, had burned the spire of St. Paul's; several times he speaks with rueful humor of the noble tower ignobly flattened on top. But he loved the great cathedral, the focus of city life; its churchyard was the center for many fascinating bookstalls and printshops festooned with engravings. Eastward lay the handsome Exchange; farther along, the rich goldsmiths' shops in Cheapside; still farther, Julius Caesar's Tower. To the west stood Ludgate Prison from whose grated windows came the cry, "Bread, for the Lord's sake!"; to the south were the river, its wharves enlivened by the shouts of wherrymen, and the great London Bridge built high with shops and dwellings and carrying a surging traffic. Westward, bordering the shore, toward Westminster lay the spacious houses of great noblemen. Dekker had scarcely exchanged his baby's gown for breeches at the time when James Burbage opened in Moorfields, north of the city, the first building in England devoted solely to the theatrical entertainment of the public and called, with propriety, "The Theatre" (1576). In the following year two others, the Curtain and the Blackfriars, began to compete with it; and thenceforward the London populace enjoyed the excitement of drama in abundance.

The city, then, offered violent contrasts of poverty and splendor, of ugliness and beauty. By modern standards it was compact and, although not easily traversed, small enough for Dekker to know all its parts. It was at once the nation's capital and a rapidly growing mart, whose merchants were seeing new opportunities in Muscovy, Morocco, the East Indies, and Virginia. Therefore, it was increasingly visited by foreign sailors, financiers, and diplomats. But, apart from its daily intensity and seasonal variety of life, the young Dekker felt his country's pulse of love and fear at this, its very heart.

With all his countrymen, he gloried in Sir Francis Drake's safe return from the circumnavigation (1580); he felt the people's anxiety about Queen Elizabeth's projected marriage to the Duke of Anjou and their fear of the plots against her life (1581); and he shared their grief for the death of Sir Philip Sidney (1586). For both Protestant and Catholic Englishmen these years of the 1580's brought intense anticipation and anxiety. When Mary, Queen of Scots, was executed in 1587, Elizabeth had reigned for twenty-nine years; but since her accession, hardly any crisis she had passed seemed worse to her than this one.

Thomas Dekker, fifteen or sixteen in that year, was old enough to understand why Elizabeth recoiled from sending Mary to the block; and he was also old enough to exult when Drake burned Spanish ships in Cadiz harbor. It is probably hard for us to exaggerate the effect on an imaginative young Protestant Londoner of the defeat of the Armada in 1588. Providence assuredly had intervened to preserve Elizabeth and her people. The emotions generated by the Armada crisis must be ranked as potent influences in forming the mind of Thomas Dekker.

III   *Young Manhood*

Assuming that Dekker was born in 1572, that he left grammar school around sixteen or seventeen years of age, and that his first work as a professional writer does not precede the first mention (1598) of him in Henslowe's *Diary* by more than four or five years, we discover a gap from the years 1588 or 1589 to 1593—a span of four or five years. We may, of course, suppose that Dekker entered apprenticeship to a trade during that time, or even that, young as he was, he began at once to offer his literary talents to the companies of actors. We have no *documentary* evidence as to what he did; but it is not true that we have no evidence at all. Dekker's constant references to the sea and sailors; his frequent allusions to "Dutch lantskops and drolleries" (genre painting); his fairly accurate use of Dutch as stage dialect;[4] his repetition of words like *hoy, dorp, frow,* and *skipper* in tracts as well as in plays; his allusions to Dutch towns and tavern customs; his use of German literary themes in a way that suggests his reading of books not yet available in English (specifically, the stories of Fortunatus and Friar Rush)—when all of these are combined with his constant sympathy for the plight of soldiers and an obvious (if not extensive) knowledge of the technicalities of navigation, arms, and warfare, it becomes a genuinely strong probability that Dekker spent a few years of his youth in some kind of service that took him to the Netherlands. Because he plainly admits never having been a soldier,[5] we are left to suppose that he either had been a sailor or had had duties that often took him to sea. His vocabulary of nautical terms is larger and more technical than a landsman could acquire unless by purposeful reading; images of the sea and navigation recur so often in his works as to seem the natural result of memories. Together, these evidences indicate actual experience of sea life.

No record of Dekker's marriage has yet been discovered. However, the late Professor F. P. Wilson found baptismal records for three children of a "Thomas Dycker" (or "Dyker") in the parish of St. Giles, Cripplegate, for the years 1594, 1598, and 1602. If Dekker were married at twenty or twenty-one—in 1592 or 1593—the birth dates of the children fit well enough. Mary, wife of Thomas "Deckers," was buried from St. James's, Clerkenwell, in 1616; if again this is the right Thomas, the unfortunate husband was then in King's Bench prison for debt. There is, of course, no certainty about how many times the dramatist was married; but, if Mary were his wife, then he was wed at least twice; for at his death his wife's name is given as Elizabeth. Between 1603 and 1613 he apparently moved from St. Giles's to the suburban parish of St. James's, nearer to the Red Bull Theater.

IV *The Dramatist*

The first unquestionable documentary record of the existence of the poet Dekker is made by Philip Henslowe, keeper of a business journal now called his *Diary,* in entries of January 8 and 15, 1598. He records payments to Dekker for writing *Phaethon,* a play now lost. Henslowe was engaged in several activities, such as iron-founding and money-lending, besides the one which has made him immensely important to the history of the Elizabethan drama—financing companies of actors, especially the Lord Admiral's Men. Professors R. T. Rickert and R. A. Foakes, who have recently edited *Henslowe's Dairy,* have tried to redress the financier's reputation, which has generally been that of an illiterate oppressor of hackwriters. These scholars appear to be right; the *Diary* does not show that he hounded his poets to jail or that he really ruined the Lord Admiral's Men by buying only trash at the lowest rates for production. As Henslowe is almost our only source of exact information about the commercial theater, the argument may seem circular. But it is altogether probable that he paid the standard price for the manuscript of a new play—about six pounds (perhaps between $250 and $300 in purchasing power today).

His recorded relations with Dekker much resemble those with "Harey" Chettle, "Benjamin" Jonson, Anthony Munday, and four or five others who provided the frequently changing fare by which the Lord Admiral's Men drew Londoners first to the Rose Theater in Southwark, then to the Fortune in Moorfields. If it seems that Dekker had a precarious existence between 1598 and late 1604, when he is last mentioned in the *Diary,* his career was probably no more comfortable before his connection with Henslowe; and certainly it was worse afterwards. The fault lay, primarily, in the theatrical system itself and, secondarily, in the occurrence of events beyond any man's control: the occasional severity of the plague and the revival of the boy companies (competitors of the adult companies) in the favor of the élite of London. Shakespeare, in *Hamlet* (II.2.341–379), has clearly told us how the Lord Chamberlain's Men felt the pressure of that competition.

Henslowe does not record the names of playwrights earlier than 1598; but his theatrical financing began at least in 1594.

It is reasonable to conjecture that Dekker was a contributor to the
Lord Admiral's Company repertory some years before 1598.
Whether for Henslowe or not, Dekker surely must have begun as
a dramatist a good deal earlier than 1598. And there are several
reasons for this supposition: First, it is incredible that a novice
in playwriting should have been competent to fabricate, wholly
or in part, fifteen plays in one year, as Henslowe records that
Dekker did in 1598. Secondly, Dekker's writings nowhere reveal
an intimate acquaintance with any occupation other than literature (except those of soldiers and sailors), and his dedication to
literature probably began with his aptness in school, though it
may have been interrupted by nautical experience. And, thirdly,
the belief that his early plays are now lost is supported by such
minor evidence as Jonson's caustic remark in *Poetaster*
(III.4.3) that "Hee ha's one of the most over-flowing ranke wits
in [London]," as well as by the reliable attribution to Dekker in
1653 of *The Jew of Venice,* a play which probably had at least a
chronological relation to Shakespeare's *Merchant of Venice* commonly dated 1596–1597.[6]

Henslowe had, by 1598, come to value Dekker highly enough to
lend the Admiral's Men forty shillings to obtain the playwright's
discharge from the Counter Prison for debtors, and he occasionally lent Dekker money in 1598 and 1599.[7] Dekker disappears from the *Diary* after September 6, 1600, until January
12, 1602, with the single exception of a record of payment to
Dekker and Chettle for *King Sebastian of Portugal* in April and
May, 1601. In 1602, however, Henslowe records Dekker's aston-
ishing productivity: his alteration of two older plays, his unaided composition of two, and his collaboration with from one
to four other writers on four plays, as well as his composition of
the prologue and epilogue for a ninth. Very likely this activity
is really typical of Dekker's years between 1594 and 1603. The
year 1602 also saw the publication of *Satiromastix* and *Blurt,
Master Constable;* although the latter appeared anonymously, it
is beyond question in large part Dekker's.

Satiromastix may well indicate the major reason for Dekker's
disappearance from *Henslowe's Diary* in late 1600 and 1601, for
the play climaxed a dramatists' feud, called the "Stage Quarrel,"
or "War of the Theaters"—a matter in which Henslowe was not

directly concerned, although Dekker was. The present sketch of Dekker's career does not require a detailed account of the origins of the quarrel, but merely a statement of the essential facts about it. In 1600 or a little earlier, the revival of the two leading companies of boy actors, the Children of the Chapel Royal (or Blackfriars Boys) and the Children of St. Paul's Chapel led to important changes in the theatrical world. The presentation of plays in the evening in smaller auditoriums at rates of admission about three times higher than those for the public theaters understandably created a more élite audience in which courtiers, students at the Inns of Court, and other youthful sophisticates predominated.

The consequent loss of clientele at the public theaters was painful to the adult companies of actors. The directors of the two boy companies felt that, to hold their special audience, they needed a repertory of comedies which should be gayly satiric in tone; and, to provide such work, they found a number of willing or eager writers, some experienced, some relatively new. Men with a taste for satire naturally sought this opportunity, notably Thomas Nashe, George Chapman, Jonson, and John Marston. Though friends at first, Jonson and Marston began to jibe at each other's style and personality. But Jonson's imprudent arrogance also led him to sneer at the crudities of popular drama and at the ignorance of its playwrights. How personal he was in these criticisms is not known, but he certainly antagonized several rivals, notably Shakespeare and Dekker. In return, Marston scored some telling blows against Jonson's conceit. These exchanges in a half dozen plays of 1599–1601 greatly amused the audience at the Blackfriars (Jonson's preserve) and at St. Paul's Theater. The climax was reached in 1601 when Jonson's *Poetaster,* attacking Marston and Dekker, was effectively answered, or perhaps anticipated, by Dekker's *Satiromastix,* produced both by the boys of St. Paul's and at the Globe by Shakespeare's company. Jonson gave up the fight, and the war was over.

Dekker's part in the "War of the Theaters," he protested, was to defend his reputation against gratuitous, personal attack. Jonson's picture of him as Demetrius Fannius is a compound of poverty, stupidity, and venality; Demetrius writes slander against any man for pay. But apart from Jonson's disparagement in private conversation of Dekker, Munday, Thomas Middleton, and other "leane-witted Poetasters," which certainly reached his victims by oral report, it is not apparent that he published lampoons of Dekker (before *Poetaster*) that are easily recognizable today.[8] There may be considerable truth in Jonson's sneer, through the mouth of Horace, that Dekker was employed by rival companies to prepare a hurried caricature of Jonson-Horace when for some reason Marston-Crispinus could not provide one.

However, we cannot fill the interval of about sixteen months —the autumn of 1600 and all of 1601—with three plays, *Sebastian of Portugal, Blurt, Master Constable,* and *Satiromastix.* Dekker could not have lived on the proceeds from these three. We are left, it seems, with the alternatives of supposing that Henslowe failed to record his payments to Dekker (but fullness in the payments to other playwrights opposes this idea) or that the plays which Dekker wrote for other companies during these months have largely disappeared or have wrongly been assumed to date from a later time. It seems a reasonable guess that during these months he was supplying a part, perhaps a major part, of the repertory of the Paul's Boys. Although the boy companies did not perform so constantly as the adult actors and, therefore, did not require so many new plays, Dekker's need for income could not have diminished. A less likely alternative is that Dekker may have written also for the Lord Chamberlain's Men or for other adult companies.

We have noted that he returned to full activity for Henslowe in January, 1602, despite the fact that the Paul's Boys were still flourishing. Consequently, it is a little surprising that Henslowe did not record any payments to Dekker in January and February of 1603. March of that year proved a dire month for London: Queen Elizabeth died on March 24; but the theaters had already been closed by ordinance on March 19 because of an alarming increase in the plague. Except for two periods totaling less than three weeks, the theaters remained closed until April, 1604. Acting companies might find some little work in the provinces, but playwrights were in no demand at all. Dekker, however, received a commission to compose part of the speeches to be pronounced at London's official greeting of King James (an event long postponed because of the epidemic); another fortunate contributor was Ben Jonson. The show, called *The Magnificent Entertainment Given to King James,* was published in 1604 from a manuscript furnished by Dekker. Jonson had earlier published his share.

By what means Dekker provided subsistence for his family and himself during most of 1603 is likely to remain a matter for sheer speculation. All that we can be sure of is that he had begun, by October or November, the writing of prose tracts, his first series of plague pamphlets. *The Wonderful Year* was published in December, 1603, or early in 1604. Although it begins with a contrast of England's deep sorrow for Elizabeth with its joy for the peaceful accession of James, its dominant theme is a solemn warning that the plague is a divine punishment for the people's sins. This pamphlet was followed by *News from Gravesend,* in the same vein of religious admonition about the plague.

In April, 1604, the theaters reopened. Sometime before March 14 of that winter, Henslowe made the last payment to dramatists that he recorded in the *Diary:* five pounds to Dekker and Middleton for *The Honest Whore* (Part I) to be acted by the Prince's Men.[9] The play must have been popular with audiences and readers, for it reached publication, probably through Dekker's initiative, at the end of 1604 and was republished three times in the next eleven years. Naturally, Dekker soon provided the actors, possibly the Prince's company, with Part II which was wholly his own work. It may have been staged in late 1604 or in 1605; its connections with Part I surely imply a close sequence. While Part II, presumably, was also popular, Dekker did not sell a copy to the publisher until 1608; and, strangely, it was not printed until 1630.

After the final entry by Henslowe relating to Dekker in 1604, we are left with the successive dates of publication of tracts and plays as our chief guide to Dekker's career. As we look over the record for the next eight years, certain facts outline Dekker's activity: (1) In 1604–1605 he collaborated with Middleton, then with John Webster. (2) The collapse of the Paul's Boys in 1606 and apparently a quarrel with the Prince's Men closed these two outlets for the playwright. Though other companies were, of course, acting, Dekker now engaged in writing tracts. (3) Around 1609–1612, he probably wrote more than one Lord Mayor's show and was attempting to return, at least occasionally, to playwriting just prior to his long imprisonment for debt, which began in 1613. These stages of his life require closer inspection.

In 1604, when the theaters were permitted to reopen after the long seige of plague, Dekker was about thirty-two, still in early middle-age by Elizabethan standards and probably fully vigorous. His expressed contempt for drunkards[10] and his religious nature justify the opinion that he was habitually a temperate man. Physically, he may have been ready for the best work of his career, but he probably suffered disquiet and even discouragement as he observed the signs of change in the world of the theater. There had been some regrouping among the adult companies; Ned Alleyn retired in 1604, and others, like Dekker's friends Thomas Downton and Robert Shaa, either had died or planned to retire. The rivalry between boys' companies and adult actors was now resumed. On the surface, the fact seemed to offer a better market for the playwright; and, as already noted, Dekker apparently tried to serve both the Paul's Boys and Henslowe's companies. With Middleton he collaborated on *The Honest Whore*, Part I, and *The Roaring Girl* for the Prince's Men, and he wrote *Sir Thomas Wyatt*[11] with Webster for the Queen's Company. Again with Webster, he composed *Westward Ho!* and *Northward Ho!* for the Paul's Boys.

But a new taste for satiric realism in comedy had begun to rule the theaters, cynicism rather than pessimism permeated tragedy—a mode of drama which Dekker always avoided—and tragicomedy was developing new sophistications of attitude and emphasis. In a brief but spectacular career in the theater, John Marston had been giving impetus to all these changes, and Ben Jonson lent the force of his personality and intelligence to satiric comedy and tragedy. Middleton, Chapman, and, for a time, Shakespeare proved to be successful recruits to these new trends. Plays like Marston's *The Malcontent* and *The Dutch Courtesan,* Middleton's *The Phoenix,* Jonson's *Volpone,* Shakespeare's *Measure for Measure* and *Othello,* and Cyril Tourneur's *The Revenger's Tragedy*—despite their continuity with the past through dramatic conventions—reveal an altered feeling and spirit.

[27]

Dekker tried to adapt to the new way of interpreting life, particularly that of London.[12] Silly intrigues of lewd citizens and their wives constitute much of the action in *Westward Ho!*; but neither Webster nor Dekker was by nature or training inclined to satire, and their comedy lacks pungency. Jonson, Marston, and Chapman then wrote *Eastward Ho!* as a high-spirited, successful travesty of middle-class Puritanism for the Blackfriars Boys and as a sort of rejoinder to *Westward Ho!*. The response by Dekker and Webster to *Eastward Ho!* was *Northward Ho!*. But its satire, apart from the amusing sketch of Chapman as Bellamont, is feeble. A citizen's wife, victim of slanderous intrigue by two gallants, finally triumphs when one of them has his own wife seduced by the other, who by trickery is then made to marry a courtesan. An effect of farce rather than satire is the essence of the play. I conclude that Dekker, whether collaborating with Middleton or Webster, did not really adapt to the vogue of satire.

A momentous event, the Gunpowder Treason in November, 1605, gave an unexpected soberness, at least momentarily, to the English dramatists. Dekker's genuine feelings about the national escape from disaster are expressed in his versified invective, *The Double PP.*, against the Pope, Catholics, and Jesuits, which he completed within a month after the discovery of the plot. Once that potboiler was in print, he composed what is one of his most impressive plays, a "Drammatical Poem," *The Whore of Babylon*. Precisely because he had put his most intense patriotism and highest conception of poetry into it, he was the more indignant that the Prince's Men suppressed or altered some parts. In his preface, *Lectori,* in the quarto of 1606, Dekker implies that, during his enforced absence, the actors had distorted it; at last, says Dekker, his offspring speaks in print as he had intended it to do.

The deduction seems safe that a sharp clash with the Prince's Company provoked these statements, and that part of the result is Dekker's turning from playwriting to tract-writing, which (as far as can be told from the record) entirely occupied him from about mid–1606 to about 1610 or later. A by-product of his anger against the Prince's Company could be the uniformly bitter tone of his references to actors in these tracts. Another by-product is his sale of two play manuscripts to printers, *The Whore of Babylon* in 1607 and *The Honest Whore,* Part II, in 1608.

V *Tract Writer*

The titles of the tracts may be seen in the Bibliography, and some analysis of the literary quality of the series is attempted in a later chapter. All that need be said here is that Dekker probably hoped to capture to some degree the attention of London as Thomas Nashe had gained it fifteen years before. In fact, there were good reasons for thinking another Nashe might succeed. Although in 1599 the Archbishop of Canterbury had decreed the end of formal verse satire and had commanded the books of the satirists to be burned, the spirit of satire had moved readily to the theater. But no one was at that time writing the prose tract aimed at a wide audience and making a wide sweep with its moralistic satire. Volumes of characters, as produced by Joseph Hall and Sir Thomas Overbury, were a highly specialized and somewhat monotonous form. The prose writers who catered to the popular taste were chiefly older pedestrian fellows like Barnabe Riche, Gervase Markham, and Nicholas Breton. Dekker's instinct was right: there was an opportunity for a prose satirist.

Dekker, however, appears never to have attained the reputation or success of Nashe, and the reasons probably lie in his own temperament. He usually varies between a homiletic tone and a facetiousness which often is not hilarious. His style (as is also true of Nashe) must carry the improvised or conventional substance of the fantastic satire; but Dekker's, though at times vivid, lacks Nashe's inexhaustible verve. From the bibliographical history of the tracts in 1606–1612, I infer that they sold well enough to encourage both Dekker and the publishers; and one of them, of course, went through many redactions under four titles: *Lantern and Candlelight, O per se O, Villainies Discovered,* and *English Villainies.* Under the commercial conditions of popular literature at that time, we may reasonably infer that Dekker did not live better than he had when writing for Henslowe, if, indeed, he lived as well.[13]

VI *1610 and After*

There is an ominous, and at present, inexplicable, blank in the record of Dekker's publication in 1610 and 1611. The single play of these two years is *The Roaring Girl*, the printer's copy of which was in Dekker's handwriting; but its date of production was about six years earlier. Conjecturally, we can assign a number of plays to this interval; for example, topical references to France and to the Bermudas support the date of 1610–1611 for *If This Be Not a Good Play*. But for other plays the speculations are too weakly founded to deserve mention. The dearth is almost as great in 1612. One play and a Lord Mayor's show are all for which we have any evidence. In January, 1613, Dekker had completed and sold *A Strange Horse-race*. Soon thereafter began the saddest affliction known to have befallen any Elizabethan dramatist: Dekker was confined for debt in the King's Bench Prison from 1613 to 1619, "almost seven years together," he says. They were probably his forty-first to his forty-eighth years.

A few events during this generally barren period should be mentioned. During late 1615, Dekker completed a poem, *The Artillery Garden;* it was copyrighted by the publisher on November 29, and apparently dated 1616. On July 24, 1616, Mary, wife of "Thomas Deckers," was buried in St. James's parish, Clerkenwell, northwest of the city. As Clerkenwell was also the site of the Red Bull Theater built around 1606, it is to be inferred that, if "Deckers" was in fact the dramatist, he had moved from St. Giles, close to the Fortune, to be closer to the Red Bull where the Queen's Company (formerly Worcester's) performed till 1617. The move may have been made about 1610. If so, one would also assume that between 1610 and 1612—the relatively blank period in the chronology—Dekker may have resumed his writing for the actors (but not for the Prince's Men).

In 1616, Dekker addressed two letters from prison (one on September 12), to an old and friendly acquaintance, the well-to-do actor Ned Alleyn, who had retired from acting in 1604. One letter explains why Dekker has dedicated a eulogistic poem to Alleyn; the other recommends to Alleyn's help the son of a fellow-prisoner. Another edition of *O per se O* was printed in 1616, with some amplifications by the author, under the title *Villainies Discovered by Lantern and Candlelight*. Predictably, of course, Dekker tried to turn his incarceration to some profit by moralized descriptions of the evils of prison life. These take the shape of essays and characters published in *Villainies* and the collections ascribed to Overbury (1616) and to Geffray Mynshul (1617) (see Bibliography). Of other work probably done in the King's Bench, only *Dekker's Dream,* copyrighted on October 11, 1619, can be identified; it was published in 1620 after the poet had been released, his hair turned white from the miseries of seven years.[14]

By what means his release was procured we do not know. We can be sure, however, that only a man stalwart of body and spirit could have emerged, as Dekker did, to take up again the struggle of living by purveying to the actors. Unquestionably his religious faith had grown humbler and stronger during the bitter, endless waiting; his Bible had been his support. His intimate knowledge of the Bible is most evident, of course, in the *Dream* and in the second series of tracts, which began five years after his release.

On emerging from prison, Dekker found that new poets had established themselves in the theatrical life of London. Among the practicing dramatists John Fletcher's prestige was supreme, for Ben Jonson had temporarily withdrawn from the theater. The King's Men monopolized Fletcher's skill, but drew occasionally upon Middleton and others. William Rowley and Nathan Field, actor-dramatists, were younger leaders in the theater. Philip Massinger and John Ford doubtless had begun playwriting during the time of Dekker's imprisonment, but no definite ascriptions to them are recorded. Of course, a number of veterans, such as Heywood, Webster, and John Day, were still on hand.

As is usually the case after the death of a sovereign, the passing of Queen Anne in March, 1619, was followed by changes; for her Company, formerly the Earl of Worcester's and a patron of Dekker, was unable to keep its identity and dissolved. The former Lord Admiral's—Prince Henry's Company, now the Palsgrave's, was still keeping in high repute the stage of the Fortune. But probably, despite the lapse of years, Dekker would not willingly apply to it. With recruits from the dissolved Queen's Company, one other strong company, Prince Charles's Men, was playing at the Red Bull. It is significant that in the interval between

[*31*]

1619 and 1625 (the latter another year of dreadful plague) Dekker is known to have collaborated on four plays for Prince Charles's Men.[15]

In 1621 or 1622 a reorganized Lady Elizabeth's Company, which began to play at the private theater called the "Phoenix" in Drury Lane, performed two other plays by Dekker, although it is not certain that one of them was originally written for the group. It is a reasonable supposition that during this span of years Dekker wrote, alone or in collaboration, a number of plays whose titles only are known to us without ascription to him or which have been completely lost. Reading Professor C. J. Sisson's account of the way Dekker, Ford, Rowley, and Webster assembled *Keep the Widow Waking*[16] reveals not only the methods of commercial collaboration, but the sturdiness of Dekker's personality. He admits, in court, to having seen the play several times and to having commended it, though moderately. It was a good show, and he was not ashamed of it.

The year 1625 was made epochal by the death of King James on March 27 and by the worst epidemic of plague since 1603. Once more the actors were disorganized and the theaters closed. Once more unfortunate Dekker, now about fifty-three, sought to use London's disaster for moral and pecuniary purposes. *A Rod for Runaways,* written about the end of July, is not one of his better tracts because its objective is not clear. It rebukes the callous Londoners who have fled the city and portrays their misery at being unable to find a refuge among the cruel, doltish countryfolk; but it then describes, rather perfunctorily, the afflictions of those left in London. We may doubt that it sold widely, if conditions were as Dekker described them. He did not soon follow it with another.

How Dekker lived during the next year and a half is not apparent. The theaters opened again in December, 1625, and doubtless he had prepared for the event. But we have no publications until 1628, and it may be that these three or four years were his last, futile attempt to eke out a living by playwriting. From the discovery that Dekker was twice indicted for recusancy, once in December, 1626, and again in March, 1628, F. P. Wilson makes the very credible inference that Dekker had to avoid arrest for debt by staying away from church (officers commonly sought their victims at the church doors on Sundays). Since Dekker's deep faith and conformity cannot be doubted, this explanation of his absence from church is surely the right one. In 1628 he published two tracts and a Lord Mayor's show; in 1629, one tract and the succeeding Lord Mayor's show.

In 1630 the plague revived again, though without a tenth of the mortality that had scourged London in 1625. The virulence was great enough, however, to cause thousands to escape from the city. Once again Dekker seized the opportunity, as he had done twice before, and produced two pamphlets of religious admonition to the citizens. In the same year he sold a play which he had perhaps first written ten years earlier, as well as a novella, and in 1631 he sold another play of uncertain date.[17]

In 1632, Dekker's popular tract, *The Bellman of London,* now revised and under its latest title, *English Villainies,* was equipped with an epistle which gives his age as three score. In the dedication which he had provided for *Match Me in London* in the previous year he had spoken of his voice as decaying with age. It is evident that in 1619, at the time he wrote *Dekker's Dream,* he longed for release from the burden of an endless struggle for subsistence. Release came in 1632. He was buried in the parish of St. James's, Clerkenwell, on August 25. The church courts recorded that his widow Elizabeth renounced administration of his estate on September 4. Professor Mark Eccles, who discovered this fact, remarks: "From the renunciation of administration it may be inferred that Dekker died in debt."[18] In short, there was no estate to administer.

We may end this sad history with the reflection that there was something lacking in Dekker which makes for material success. A purveyor of innocent amusement mingled with moral instruction, a man profoundly sympathetic with the poor and oppressed, a lover of God and country, Dekker should have received better treatment from the world. If there is such a thing as bad fortune, Dekker unquestionably suffered from it more than most. But a greater poet like Jonson could live upon patrons; a shrewder businessman like Shakespeare could enter a successful organization. Dekker was a writer who seemed inevitably fated for a literary career but who was denied the practicality that makes writing an endurable way of life.

CHAPTER 2

Dekker's Drama: Independent Work

M ORE than with most dramatists of the English Renaissance, it is necessary to begin a consideration of Dekker's
plays with a reminder of how thoroughly this playwright is sustained by the native dramatic tradition. *The Shoemaker's
Holiday* (1599), the most familiar of his works to twentieth-
century readers, may be somewhat misleading in this respect;
for, despite its romantic love-theme, this comedy is likely to be
regarded as marking an advance in realism in its depiction of
bourgeois life. Actually, the advance was being made, then
and in the next decade, by Ben Jonson and such younger satiric
dramatists as Marston and Middleton. In contrast, *The Shoemaker's Holiday* and Dekker's better plays continued throughout
his career to rely on the conventions and devices which he had
learned in the early 1590's; and these have little affinity with
tragic or satiric realism. Although partitioning the English dramatic tradition into morality, romantic, comic, and chronicle
elements may seem at first a needless, pedantic method (so closely
are the conventions woven together), such division may nevertheless prove helpful as a preliminary analysis leading to a critical appraisal of the plays.

A word of caution, however, needs to be spoken. "Naïve and
preposterous" is likely to be our judgment about any play such
as *Patient Grissil* in which a medieval saint's legend and the
taming-of-the-shrew theme are so oddly mingled. But so to dismiss the play is really to reveal our own unfamiliarity with the
conventions Dekker has employed. Rather, our judgment should
estimate primarily the truth inherent in the author's structure
of values. Of course, the dramatist makes his statement by fusing
story, verbal symbols and connotations, theatrical devices, and

modes of acting; and his skill in combining these media determines the force of his utterance. However, in the Elizabethan age the media themselves had either originated in, or for generations been associated with, the philosophic and religious beliefs which the dramatist and his audience held in common. As readers, we must understand the full significance of the conventions if we are to gauge the playwright's success. An obvious example of traditional significance is the flat characterization, derived from morality plays and interludes, which Jonson, for instance, relied on to express moral truth in *Volpone*.

If this conception is true, and if Dekker seems to have handled the conventional elements effectively for the Elizabethan audience, our response to the archaic means he used is less important than the effect he produced. And this effect we must keep in mind. The stamina undoubtedly felt in many of Dekker's plays grows out of his command of conventions which are now foreign. The charge of "carelessness" too often laid on him by critics arises partly from their failing to recognize his full reliance on dramatic and histrionic tradition.

I *Elizabethan Dramatic Conventions*

" 'Tis out of Fashion to bring a Divell upon the Stage," Dekker remarked in his tract *News from Hell* (1606). But some two years later, in *If This Be Not a Good Play, the Devil Is in It,* he not only brought devils on stage, but represented damned souls tormented in Hell-fire. The explicit purpose of such a spectacle in *If This Be Not a Good Play* will be discussed later in this chapter; at this point we may pause only to note that Dekker did not exploit the mere fireworks of Medieval drama in other plays that have survived. But so consistently did he utilize elements of the mystery, morality, and interlude traditions that his plays demonstrate better than any other dramatist's the continuity of Medieval and Renaissance drama. What is more important, we are led to the conclusion that his fidelity to these conventions was caused not by his clinging to familiar ways indolently or unthinkingly, but by his conviction that the conventions most forcefully served to express the basic truths of life. The same belief prompted Thomas Heywood's complaint against the narrowed scope of Stuart drama.[1]

[*35*]

Therefore, in spite of the fact that Dekker's reliance on ancient conventions may sometimes appear routine and not very significant (as, for instance, his use of doggerel verse for a moralizing summary in Part II of *The Honest Whore*), we must keep in mind the original potency of the tradition. The audience in the public theaters of 1600 included a considerable number of people who had also, some years earlier, witnessed performances of mystery plays at Coventry, Chester, Kendal, or elsewhere; and, no doubt, nearly all of the audience had attended moralities and interludes.[2] To them, the conventions of religious drama were vital and significant, not amusing archaisms. The universally important contest of God with Satan for the soul of man gave to native dramatic tradition an impact we can scarcely imagine. Because Dekker, as man and as dramatist, grew up in what we may call "the last era of the Medieval drama" and believed the doctrine which that drama aimed to teach, he naturally utilized its resources as fully as possible. In doing so, of course, he also obeyed the Classical maxim to mingle the useful with the delightful.

As a result, Dekker's plays furnish the historian of drama with examples of more than twenty ancient conventions of theme, characterization, and theatrical devices.

I list the more important themes with the name of one play in which each theme occurs: the saint's legend (*The Virgin Martyr*); the testing of heroic virtue (*Patient Grissil*); the detection of evil counselors of the prince (*Patient Grissil*); the victory of patience over persecution (Part II of *The Honest Whore*); social satire in the Medieval tradition (*The Whore of Babylon*); and the peasantry used to voice justice and truth (*Sir Thomas Wyatt*).

Among conventions of characterization are the shrewish wife as comic figure (Part I of *The Honest Whore*); the Judas-like betrayer of his master (*Sir Thomas Wyatt*); personified ideas, such as Time, in conjunction with historical persons and events (*The Whore of Babylon*); personifications of moral forces, good or evil (*The Virgin Martyr*); persons who signify classes, not individuals (*If This Be Not a Good Play*); human persons who embody a single virtue or vice, each receiving his proper reward (*The Wonder of a Kingdom*); "depersonalization," that is, temporary abandonment of a character's individuality permitting him to voice a point of view more eloquently (*The Witch of Edmonton*); and the introduction of superhuman beings (*The Virgin Martyr*).

Finally, among theatrical and stage devices: formal debate between two moral points of view, with implicit appeal to the audience for decision (Part II of *The Honest Whore*); a scene of moral judgment to end the play, that is, a trial (*Old Fortunatus*); the formalizing of a motif, as in a dance of courtesans, for temptation (*If This Be Not a Good Play*); or as in a shift to contrasting expression, the use of archaic verse to utter forgiveness for the prodigal or to summarize the moral (Part II of *The Honest Whore*); showing executions on stage (*Old Fortunatus*); and the use of symbolic properties like the Mountain of Truth or the Tree of Vice (*The Whore of Babylon*).

The preceding features, which we may inclusively call "morality" conventions, have been named first because their moral implications were important to Dekker. However, it is clear that, both historically and in Dekker's drama, these conventions were adapted to general utility in chronicle play, comedy, and romance. An obvious example is the shrewish wife Viola, in Part I of *The Honest Whore*. No doubt she is a descendant of Noah's wife in the mystery plays. But Plautine comedy also presented the Elizabethans with the type of the tyrannical wife; and it is reasonable to suppose that sheer truth regarding actual English life helped to create the characters of the shrews in Elizabethan and Jacobean comedy. In summary, the "morality" conventions are to be understood as employed by Dekker whenever they are appropriate in any of the genres, and the following discussion does not repeat them.

Chronicles, or history plays, constitute a large proportion of the drama of the 1590's; and Henslowe's *Diary* indicates that Dekker wrote a good many of them. But of all this work we have only the garbled text of *Sir Thomas Wyatt* (1602?), said by its publisher to be a collaboration between Dekker and John Webster. *Wyatt* may be a combination of Parts I and II of *Lady Jane*, mentioned by Henslowe in 1602, or of parts of these plays. To the extent that it is by Dekker, as yet very hard to determine, it shows his use of a well-established theme of chronicle drama: a simplified, idealized, patriotic character opposed tragically by a group of ambitious, factious lords. The patriot is a staunch defender of Tudor ideas of sovereignty, including those of primogeniture and divine right. As defender of political truth, Wyatt is of the same type as Woodstock, hero of the anonymous play called by that name, and of Gaunt, in Shakespeare's *Richard II*.

As is often true in chronicles, the other characters in *Wyatt* fall into groups, chiefly the pair of ambitious nobles, Northumberland and Suffolk, supporters of Lady Jane as successor to Henry VIII, and the larger, rival faction which supports Princess Mary. In quality the members of the factions need not be, and are not, sharply distinguished from each other. Other political elements of the realm are represented by such groups of anonymous characters as soldiers and peasants. Like the gardeners in *Richard II*, the countrymen in *Wyatt*, when most significant (II.1), speak with the voice of *Res Publica* in the interludes; but they are otherwise just choric representatives of the masses, or "common conditions." Besides disorder, another aspect of the evil of civil conflict—the suffering visited on the whole nation—is expressed through choric laments by groups of noblewomen. Some of these conventions occur also in other Dekker plays.

In his handling of the comic elements of drama, Dekker is equally dependent on convention. Unquestionably he had a lively sense of the droll and ludicrous in human behavior. Yet with the possible exception of Thomas Heywood, no dramatist approaching Dekker's stature draws more often on the armory of standard comic types and devices which were familiar in the public theaters of the 1580's and 1590's. Five of these traditional resources may be grouped under the heading of stock characters: the loyal, but saucy, servingman, usually labelled the "Clown," a mischief-loving young fellow or a satiric old one, disrespectful to his master, but tolerated by him (*Match Me in London*); the absurd foreigner—vaunting, cowardly Spaniard, lewd Frenchman, crude Irish footman, avaricious Dutchman, or touchy Welshman—caricatured in temperament and manners, but ridiculous chiefly because of his dialect (*Satiromastix*); the female bawd who speaks lewd double entendres (*Match Me in London*); the pert page (*Match Me in London*); and the witty young lady-in-waiting (*Patient Grissil*).

[*38*]

Whether caricatures of fops, upstart gallants, and fantastic courtiers are cited as exemplifying stock characterization or satiric themes is unimportant; in any case, Dekker introduces these comic persons, frequently making them victims of the lady-in-waiting's repartee, which, it should be said, scores more points by well-tried puns and open ridicule than by wit (*Patient Grissil*). For more biting satire, however, Dekker also sets the impudent servingman against the fops (*Match Me in London*). All readers of *Shoemaker's Holiday* remember that Dekker relishes heavy repetition of absurd phrases ("prince am I none, yet am I nobly born"), a device that is the "humor" reduced to its simplest form. Occasionally, he also introduces the mock prophecy (*The Whore of Babylon*) and the dialogue with Echo (*If This Be Not a Good Play*).

Lastly, the conventions of romantic drama which Dekker uses are very numerous. He dramatizes folktale themes: the peasant girl and her royal lover (*Patient Grissil*); the persecuted but forgiving wife (*If This Be Not a Good Play*); long separation of parents and children (*Patient Grissil*); love at first sight (*Blurt, Master Constable*); the testing of lovers' faith in each other (*Satiromastix*); and the selfish ambition of fathers that destroys their children (*Sir Thomas Wyatt*). Among romantic characters we find the rejected lover who makes a vow of celibacy (*Shoemaker's Holiday*); in a different mood, the witty lady-in-waiting also does so (*Patient Grissil*). The villain in these plays, whether he is a revenger, a lustful king, or a tyrannical father, is converted to benevolence for the denouement (*Match Me in London*). His accomplice is also discovered to be a good man at the end (Part I of *The Honest Whore*). Characters are utilized for rather incongruous functions, becoming expositors, intriguers, or benefactors, according to the needs of major and minor plots (Part II of *The Honest Whore*). These manipulations of character might, of course, be properly placed in the category of devices.

There are many other conventional devices to be noted. Obviously, disguise is extremely common (*Shoemaker's Holiday*). For surprise or irony Dekker frequently relies on the administering of a sleeping potion (*Satiromastix*). Among the threats to the happiness of the lovers is *droit du seigneur* (*Satiromastix*).

The happy ending of their trials is signalized by several marriages, a feast, and a dance (*Satiromastix*). Magic appears in various forms (*If This Be Not a Good Play*), including witchcraft (*The Witch of Edmonton*). At times, mythical beings and spirits intervene in the action (*The Virgin Martyr*). Music is the cause or symbol of supernatural influence (*Old Fortunatus*) and also increases pathos (*Patient Grissil*). Passages of lyricism in the dialogue, written in the strains of Ovidian or Petrarchan verse, also heighten the sentiment (*Old Fortunatus*). On a lower level of dramaturgy, we find the familiar expedients of Elizabethan construction: great lapses of time (*Patient Grissil*); frequent shifts of scene (*Old Fortunatus*); and the use of the chorus—that is, prologue (*Old Fortunatus*) and the dumbshow (*The Whore of Babylon*), a device to which Dekker clings throughout his career.

The preceding lists are certainly incomplete. They will be supplemented by mention of Dekker's more artistic uses of traditional technique in the discussion of individual plays in this and in the next chapter. The intention of these analyses is to establish Dekker's major plays in their genres, then to evaluate them in broader critical fashion. The major independent plays I take to be these seven, in chronological order: *Old Fortunatus; The Shoemaker's Holiday; Satiromastix;* Part II of *The Honest Whore; The Whore of Babylon; If This Be Not a Good Play, the Devil Is in It;* and *Match Me in London.* Although Thomas Middleton collaborated with Dekker in Part I of *The Honest Whore,* Dekker's share is both large and characteristic; and Part II's development of the situations and characters of Part I practically requires that the earlier play be considered first.

II   An Exemplum for the Court: Old Fortunatus (1599)

Without question, *Old Fortunatus,* as we now have it, was written by Dekker as a parable for the moral instruction of the audience at Queen Elizabeth's court. The evidence leading to this conclusion lies in the dramatist's adaptation of the story, as well as in Henslowe's record of the steps in the composition of the play. But because the tale of Fortunatus is no longer so familiar as it once was, references to it will be more intelligible if we first review Dekker's version in the play.

The story is of the goddess Fortune's dealing with a poor man and his two sons, Ampedo and Andelocia. Finding Fortunatus asleep in a wood in Cyprus, the goddess awakens him and offers a choice of gifts—strength, health, beauty, long life, riches, or wisdom. When Fortunatus chooses riches, Fortune gives him a magic purse, always laden with ten gold pieces. Of course, it immediately enriches the father and his two sons, enabling Fortunatus to travel about the world. Meanwhile, we watch a scene in which Virtue and Vice plant trees while Fortune looks on, indifferent as to which tree flourishes. The fame of Fortunatus's wealth runs everywhere; in Babylon, the Sultan plots to discover the magic source of his visitor's gold. Fortunatus, who escapes this peril by pretending to be unaware, innocently borrows the Sultan's magic wishing hat and wishes himself at home again.

When Fortune warns him of his imminent death, Fortunatus pleads with her to exchange the purse for the gift of wisdom for his sons; she refuses. The father leaves purse and hat to be used by both sons for their common benefit. He is scarcely cold, however, before the wastrel younger son, Andelocia, forces his brother to divide the use of the prizes year by year. Taking the purse, Andelocia goes to England with the Prince of Cyprus who intends to woo Agripyne, daughter of King Athelstane. The King, intrigued by Andelocia's flaunted riches, tells Agripyne to pretend love for Andelocia, then steal the purse. By giving the youth a sleeping potion, Agripyne succeeds. Andelocia returns to Cyprus, steals the wishing hat from Ampedo, cheats some Italian jewelers of their gems, and returns to England, disguised as a jewel merchant. While bargaining with Agripyne about his wares, he suddenly clasps her and takes her to a wilderness; there he threatens to abandon her unless she will promise to marry him. As she seems fainting from thirst, Andelocia climbs an apple tree (in reality, Vice's) to pick some luscious fruit. When Agripyne complains of the hot sun, he throws her his wishing hat. Unaware of its power, she wishes she were in England and is presently snatched away—with the hat.

Meantime, Vice's apples have grown horns on Andelocia's head. Fortune comes to him, bringing with her Vice and Virtue. The contending goddesses offer him the fruits of their trees; but having been enlightened by Fortune about the cause of his horns, Andelocia repents his bad life and chooses Virtue's apples. His horns fall off. During this time, King Athelstane in England promises to marry his daughter to the Prince of Cyprus. Now Andelocia, still lusting for the purse and hat, comes back disguised as an Irish costermonger and sells Vice's apples to Agripyne and to two foolish courtiers; they all grow horns after eating the fruit. The Prince of Cyprus renounces his claims to a horned princess. Disguised anew, this time as a French doctor, Andelocia gives the courtiers a pill to remove the horns; instead of helping Agripyne, he snatches up the wishing hat and carries the princess off to Ampedo's house in England. Ampedo has come there in hopes of turning Andelocia from his prodigal life. After Andelocia has finally obtained the magic purse from Agripyne he sends her, eating an apple of Virtue to remove her horns, to find her way back to court.

His malice unsatisfied, Andelocia returns to court, preparing to enjoy more trickery. Ampedo is meanwhile unable to dissuade him from his course and burns the wishing hat. Ampedo is seized by the de-horned courtiers who, in the belief that he has the magic purse, put him in the stocks in order to extort gold from him; there he dies of grief. When Andelocia falls into their hands, he loses his purse to them, is also stocked, and then is hanged. The play ends with a short trial scene in which Vice, Virtue, and Fortune claim sovereignty over Athelstane and his court. But Vice ultimately flees, and Fortune kneels to Queen Elizabeth, the ruler of destiny, in whom Virtue finds the embodiment of herself.

This detailed summary enables us to see how Dekker shaped his source-material with a moral purpose; his play is not merely a naïve rehandling of a naïve folktale. A brief review of the relations of Dekker's plot to the work which was probably his immediate source[3]—the German *Volksbuch* "Of Fortunatus and His Purse and Wishing-Hat" (first published in 1509)—reveals some significant changes. The folktale moves slowly but clearly and presents the careers of the father and sons in sequence, so that a dramatist who planned to make two plays would have found a convenient dividing point at Fortunatus's death. However, Dekker produces a considerable overlap of the two parts; Fortunatus's death and bequeathing of the purse and hat come at the end of Act II. Contemporary readers of the *Volksbuch* probably enjoyed the story of Fortunatus's career chiefly because of the inserted episodes of murder, theft, and lust. Dekker has omitted nearly all of this material; in fact, he adapts only two events (both necessary to prepare for Andelocia's adventures): the father's encounter with the goddess Fortune and his theft of the Sultan's wishing hat. A chorus before Act II summarizes a few of Fortunatus's actions between these two episodes.

For the remaining three acts, Dekker adapts many, but not all, of Andelocia's exploits in relation to Agripyne; the chorus that precedes Act IV is an awkward device to weave in the omitted events necessary to understand the following scene. But more important than Dekker's struggle to dramatize the loose episodes in the *Volksbuch* is the change in tone at which he aimed. Partly through additional action, partly through lamentation, comment, and homily, Dekker emphasizes waste more than the other forms of vice in the careers of Fortunatus and Adelocia. The evil of prodigality, however, is a theme completely absent from the *Volksbuch*.

The process of Dekker's composition of the play could give further indications of his purpose. However, the obscurity in the theatrical origins of *Old Fortunatus* has caused problems for the historian of drama which are the most numerous among all Dekker's works. Certainly the play as we have it is Dekker's recasting and amplification of an older one, now lost, called by Henslowe *The First Part of Fortunatus* (February 3, 1596). But "First Part" implies a second part, either then existing or soon to be written, unless Henslowe's title, rather unusually, echoes the title of a lost book of the legend.[4] We know of no *Second Part;* for, when Henslowe first mentions Dekker's name in connection with the play on November 9, 1599, while recording a payment of forty shillings, he speaks of *The Whole History of Fortunatus.* Naturally, in the light of these two recorded titles, scholars have supposed that a *Second Part* may have been projected which was to deal with the adventures of Fortunatus's two sons, but that Dekker spontaneously, or at the actors' suggestion, decided to combine the father's and sons' adventures in one play, *The Whole History of Fortunatus.* On the other hand, it has been denied that Dekker wrote *The First Part,* but it has been accepted without question that he wrote *The Whole History.*

Dekker obviously eliminated some episodes used in *The First Part of Fortunatus,* yet his recasting created an unusually long play. It was finally completed by November 30, 1599, when Dekker was paid six pounds for it.[5] The next day, however, Henslowe began a new series of payments to Dekker for the altering of *The Whole History of Fortunatus* "for the Court," as he says a few days later. The play was produced before Queen Elizabeth on December 27, 1599. There had hardly been time for a performance on the stage of the Rose Theater. And it is remarkable that the play is not mentioned again by Henslowe, and that *Old Fortunatus in His New Livery* was entered in the Stationers' Register on February 20, 1600, and published in that year "as it was played before the Queen's Majesty this Christmas."[6] In the quarto are printed two prologues by Dekker, one of them (like the epilogue) designed especially for the performance at court.

From the preceding data we can see that the play as we have it was in existence only about eight weeks before Dekker or the actors sold it to the publisher, the manuscript being probably in Dekker's own hand. This very early sale and the lack of further reference by Henslowe[7] do not prove conclusively that the play in its full length was not produced publicly again, but they definitely lead to that inference. If produced, *Old Fortunatus* was perhaps cut down to more normal length and made less expensive (in December the actors had borrowed ten pounds from Henslowe to buy "things" for the performance).

In spite of the many uncertainties in the history just given, the evidence surely justifies our conclusion that *Old Fortunatus* is one of Dekker's ambitious plays, one worked on seriously and intended for a sophisticated audience. The importance of this conclusion is not lessened by our uncertainty about whether Dekker wrote *The First Part of Fortunatus* in 1595, then four years later decided to amalgamate it and the remainder of the *Volksbuch* material in one play, or whether in 1599 he combined two existent plays. We are sure that in 1599 he joined certain episodes from *The First Part of Fortunatus* with some of Andelocia's adventures. And we can be almost equally sure that Henslowe's second series of large payments was for the composition of a substantial revision of the new play, specifically the incorporation into it of the morality element—the contest between Fortune, Vice, and Virtue—rather than simply for a contribution of a Prologue and an Epilogue for the court.[8] Then we make the valid inference that Dekker, having learned that *The Whole History of Fortunatus* was intended for performance at the court, deliberately attempted to add moral gravity to the fantastic story. He expected to have at court a more thoughtful and critical audience than that of the Rose Theater.

Although C. H. Herford's analysis of the changes that Dekker made in the fable of the *Volksbuch* is complete enough,[9] his evaluation of the changes must be amended. He says that Dekker altered the character of Fortune from a fond, pampering mother (as in the source) to a stern, judicial goddess who disapproves and punishes Fortunatus's bad choice of riches. But it is not essentially the choice of riches that she condemns; it is his abuse of riches, his improvidence: "Thou hast eaten metals, and abusde my giftes,/Hast plaid the Ruffian, wasted that in ryots,/Which as a blessing I bestowed on thee" (II.2.235–237).

Second, Andelocia is displayed as the prodigal son, and his brother Ampedo, a virtuous, prudent youth, is the foil to him; whereas in the *Volksbuch,* Andelocia is envied as the lucky hero up to the last episode. Though Herford does not note the fact, the theme of evil prodigality is a favorite with Dekker throughout his life; he dwells on it in both plays and tracts. The contrast between Andelocia and Ampedo, therefore, is a parable; it is a quite definite moral preachment for Elizabeth's courtiers. Third, there is the rivalry of Fortune, Vice, and Virtue. Herford believes that, in the play as first planned, Fortune was shown as "the supreme arbiter of the world . . . in no hostile relation to moral good . . . at least tolerant of virtue."[10] Yet for purposes of compliment to Queen Elizabeth, Virtue has been personified; and her supremacy over Fortune must be shown. Hence, says Herford, a seeming incoherence of ideas exists in the play.

We cannot deny that for the modern reader the Fortune-Virtue relation has an effect of incoherence; but it is likely that the Elizabethan audience saw little or no inconsistency. In the first place, the figure of Fortune is introduced as the capricious "Queene of chaunce" who thrusts pain or pleasure on men without regard to merit, seating base cowards in honor's chair, putting an idiot's cap on virtue's head. In this view of her actions, a man's vice or virtue is quite irrelevant, because her tumbling a prince from his throne is only a more spectacular instance of caprice and not really different from a beggar's finding money in the street. Now, it is important also to see that her enjoyment of her sport is increased by her awareness of the irony in her frustrating human expectations based on merit. As a dramatic person, Fortune must be satiric, or she is little more than an annoyance.

Dekker relies on this trait of her character (I.1.65–129) and then uses a development of it which is less obvious. Fortune's sportiveness is combined with scorn for the fools who think vice can bring them lasting pleasure, as she likewise shows her contempt for fools who think virtue will bring them protection. In Act IV (1.111–227) she is presiding over a contest between Virtue and Vice for the devotion of Andelocia. It is fully consistent with her satiric attitude ("Sing and amongst your Songs, mix bitter scorne" [117]) for her to identify Vice to Andelocia as the cause of the horns he now wears and of future evils, to identify Virtue in her fool's costume, to call Andelocia "fool," and to tell him how his trial will be continued. In no way does she control his choices, although she can alter his situation in a moment. She remains entirely unpredictable, and the prodigal is entirely responsible for his moral decisions.

True, in the finale (V.2), Fortune seems momentarily severe and judicial, even angry (lines 206–223). But she performs, in fact, no judicial acts; she resigns the punishment of the evil courtiers, Longaville and Montrose, to Athelstane as she has resigned the punishment of Athelstane and Agripyne because Virtue pardoned them (224). Her acts, therefore, always remain devoid of moral quality. But as Fortune has been the major deity of the play, she is given a brief passage of solemn prophecy to speak about England's future wealth (259–260); then (her irony now being dropped) she relapses completely into the basic element of her character—blind capriciousness[11]—and she stupidly supposes that Vice is more esteemed than Virtue. She tries to refer the decision of this question to the audience, but Virtue appeals to the Queen, her own embodiment. Vice flees, and Fortune makes herself the slave of Elizabeth.

[46]

For a Renaissance audience familiar with the abundant literature and iconography of the goddess, nothing in Dekker's representation of her is inconsistent with the final triumph of Virtue over Vice or with the traditional indifference of Fortune to
moral quality in human beings. The only distinct change in her
at any time is the omission of her satiric scorn in the last scene.

I have dwelt upon this aspect of the play as the most important, for it is the element most demonstrative of Dekker's serious
theme, as it is also the most spectacular feature. Herford and
others speak of the Fortune-Vice-Virtue episodes as masque elements, implying, perhaps, frivolity of purpose in them, a
"frigid and artificial allegory."[12] But certainly in purpose and
probably in dramatic effect the Fortune episodes exemplify
what is essentially a surviving morality play, despite the exaggeration of spectacle and the omission of theological ideas. The episodes serve to introduce and deepen the evil of a specific vice,
waste.

Indeed, as Dekker sees the legend, it provides two prodigals:
old Fortunatus and Andelocia. We meet Fortunatus when he is
old but still a fool (so Echo describes him), one who has lost his
way in the forest of the world, but who yet wishes he had a little
more virtue. Involuntary fasting has made him chaste, and poverty has made him patient—"marie [,] I haue praied little, and
that makes mee [that] I still [*always*] daunce...." (I.1.18–19). Rejecting wisdom and other good gifts, he chooses riches, and Fortune scorns him: "Farewel, vaine couetous foole, thou wilt repent" (I.1.308).

Likewise, Andelocia, the true son of his father, rants against
the inequality in the world: "Art not thou mad, to see money
on Goldsmithes stalles, and none in our purses?" Ampedo speaks
the proper answer:

> But fooles haue alwaies this loose garment wore,
> Being poore themselues, they wish all others poore ...
> Fie, brother *Andelocia,* hate this madnes,
> Turne your eyes inward, and behold your soule,
> That wants more than your body: burnish that
> With glittering Vertue: and make Ideots grieue
> To see your beautious mind in wisedome shine,
> As you at their rich pouertie repine. (I.2.99–100, 125–132)

But his remonstrance has no effect. After death, Fortunatus's body is carried away by satyrs, the slaves of Fortune, to a pagan burial; yet the warning given to his sons by his unhappy death is promptly flouted by Andelocia, who "in wildness tottre[s] out his youth" (IV.1.106). Dekker tries to focus the whole lesson where Fortune introduces Andelocia to Virtue and Vice in person (IV.1). Andelocia chooses Virtue. But he relapses at once into his former folly (V.2.50–61), and his end is hanging, though with time allowed for repentance:

> *Vertue,* forgiue me, for I haue transgrest
> Against thy lawes, my vowes are quite forgot . . .
> Riches and knowledge are two gifts diuine.
> They that abuse them both as I haue done,
> To shame, to beggerie, to hell must runne. (V.2.170–171, 173–175)

Although Andelocia's end is predictable, we are surprised to see Ampedo, so often the voice of caution, dying miserably in the stocks. However, Virtue explains that he also was a fool:

> . . . Those that (like him) doe muffle
> *Vertue* in clouds, and care not how shee shine,
> Ile make their glorie like to his decline:
> He made no vse of me, but like a miser,
> Lockt vp his wealth in rustie barres of sloth . . .
> So perish they that so keepe vertue poore. (V.2.272–276, 279)

Indirectly addressing the noble audience, Virtue means that, possessed of the means to do good to the needy (the magic purse and hat), Ampedo did nothing. In short, his sin was sloth.

Old Fortunatus, then, is insistently a morality play. But it is the morality, or the interlude, in an awkward stage of change. Its elements are not fully harmonized. Charles Lamb eloquently praises the poetry of Orleans's romantic speeches; but this charm is too slight to count for much. What count are the moral preachments just analyzed, the scenes of spectacle (Fortune treading on kings as she mounts her throne; magical disappearances with the wishing hat), the intrigue at Athelstane's court, and the comedy. Irrepressible Shadow's clownage, Andelocia disguised as an Irish costermonger, the Soldan of Babylon being cozened of his wishing hat, Agripyne and her suitors wearing horns—these comic devices loudly compete with the morality play. The trouble is that they do not blend with it. Dekker's genuine earnestness in *Old Fortunatus* is partly frustrated by his employment of conventional elements of comedy and spectacle. However, the play has much more depth than has usually been found in it.

III   *A Ballad Theme:* The Shoemaker's Holiday *(1599)*

The exuberant fun of *The Shoemaker's Holiday,* which has resulted in its distinction of being one of the few Elizabethan comedies—other than Shakespeare's or Jonson's—which are frequently revived in this century, leads some critics to the conclusion that it is Dekker's masterpiece. Acknowledging the play's vitality, we gain little by quibbling about the term "masterpiece"; but to label *The Shoemaker's Holiday* "Dekker's best romantic comedy" is certainly more exact. In none of his other surviving plays does he mingle conventional comic and love-story elements so adroitly. However, to view the play as a masterpiece of realism or even as making a genuine innovation in any kind of realism is an error.

Before considering Dekker's use of romantic legend we should summarize the action of the comedy. When Rowland Lacy, prodigal nephew and heir of the Earl of Lincoln, finds himself penniless in Germany, he learns the trade of the shoemaker. After he has made his way back to London and has restored himself to his uncle's favor, he falls in love with Rose, daughter of a wealthy citizen, Sir Roger Otley, the Lord Mayor. Both his uncle and her father resolutely oppose the match as being against the interest of both families. A further complication is the English King's war against France (which king and which campaign Dekker leaves vague).[13] The Earl procures a colonelcy for Rowland; Sir Roger impresses certain tradesmen for the ranks, especially Ralph, journeyman to the master shoemaker, Simon Eyre. Ralph parts sadly from his wife Jane, the maidservant to Eyre's wife Margery.

Although the Lord Mayor has taken pains to sequester his daughter at his country home in Oldford, Rose is able to learn of Lacy's movements by sending her waiting-woman Sybil to the musters near London. Some weeks later, Lacy secretly returns from France, puts on the disguise of a Dutch shoemaker, and takes service with Eyre, replacing Ralph. Besides the fact that Lacy risks death for having deserted treasonably, Rose herself is imperilled by her father's decision to marry her to Hammon. Hammon, a citizen, has fallen in love with Rose when he encountered her near Oldford where he was hunting. However, she firmly refuses this match; Hammon, for his part, will not consent to Sir Roger's coercing his daughter into the marriage.

Meantime, Lacy helps Eyre, his master, to buy a cargo from a Dutch skipper and thus to profit greatly. Soon Eyre is elected Lord Mayor and is handsomely entertained by Otley at Oldford. Among Eyre's men on this occasion is Lacy, and Rose recognizes him. Later she summons Lacy to fit her with shoes, and thus they are able to plan elopement, with the aid of Sybil.

In the interim, the campaign in France has been suspended, and Ralph returns, crippled, to London. But he finds that Jane has left Eyre's house, driven away by Mistress Eyre's scolding. Jane has opened her own seamstress shop (unknown to Ralph) where Hammon has discovered and wooed her. When he declares that Ralph is dead, she reluctantly agrees to marry Hammon. However, when Hammon's servant brings Ralph a love-knot shoe and orders him to make a new pair for a wedding, Ralph recognizes Jane's shoe. His fellows in Eyre's shop rally to help him intercept the procession on the way to church and to claim Jane for his wife.

Firke, one of Ralph's co-workers, delivers Rose's shoe at Oldford. There he is questioned by Sir Roger who has learned that Lacy is hiding in London. At this moment, word is brought that Rose has eloped with Hans the shoemaker; and the Earl of Lincoln, who has come to inquire about his nephew from Otley, surmises that it is Lacy in disguise. However, Firke misinforms the two old men about the church where the lovers are to be married. Lacy, who has revealed himself to Eyre and induced the master and his wife to be witnesses, is married to Rose at the Savoy while the two guardians are waiting for them at St. Faith's.

Although the Earl and Lord Mayor plead to the King for a separation of the lovers, Eyre's good humor and shrewdness win the day for Lacy and Rose. The King refuses to annul the marriage; instead, he restores Lacy's honor by knighting him (thus he also increases the Earl's honor). The guardians are reconciled to the marriage, and the play ends festively with the King's consent for his prentices to eat at Eyre's banquet.

In this well-written play Dekker has used imaginatively elements from three legends in Thomas Deloney's *The Gentle Craft,* Part I, a book published apparently at the end of 1597, though no copies of the first edition have survived. The three tales include two vulgarized Medieval saints' legends: that of St. Hugh's love for St. Winifred, perhaps to be called a tragedy because of their martyrdom, and that of St. Crispine's love for St. Ursula, which ends happily with their marriage. The third legend is the career of Simon Eyre, historically a woolen-draper but made a shoemaker by Deloney—a desirable change because both Hugh and Crispine disguised themselves as shoemakers, and because the book is addressed to the "Professors of the Gentle ['noble'] Craft; of what degree soeuer."

Actually, Dekker utilizes only three story elements from the saints' lives: that Hugh and Crispine are princes; that they disguise as shoemakers; and that Crispine courts Ursula while fitting her. But the dramatist makes frequent humorous allusion to other details of their legends. On the other hand, he appropriates most of Deloney's legend of Simon Eyre, omitting only a fabliau concerning Eyre's housemaid (not Jane); yet from that he borrows the name, but not the character, of Hans the Dutchman. It is noteworthy that in Deloney's account, Eyre, although he has a quiet sense of humor, is a much soberer and more dignified person than in the play. This difference fully demonstrates Dekker's genius for characterization. He has kept the virtues of the original Eyre—industry and kindliness—and has rounded the character by adding tenderness for "my sweete lady *Madgy,*" volubility, robustious humor, and, above all, an awareness of his own absurdities: "... Feare nothing *Rose,* let them al say what they can, [*sings*] dainty come thou to me: laughest thou?" (V.1.8–9). As a recent critic says, Eyre is a "shrewd exploiter of his own eccentricities."[14]

The careful structure of the play deserves a word of praise. As counterpoint to the evil of two ambitious old men's planning marriages of advantage for their children and thus thwarting the natural love between pure, devoted young folk, Dekker intro-

[*51*]

duces the pathos of a young couple of the lower class separated by the crisis of war and reunited only after near tragedy. Besides these thematic parallels of love, youth, and fidelity, Dekker takes other pains to unify the two plots. The two male lovers are both shoemakers, one pretended, the other true; the French war threatens Lacy's love affair, but actually separates Ralph from Jane; and the same unwelcome wooer attempts to win, first Rose, then Jane. Firke, the journeyman shoemaker, a much transformed clever servant from Roman comedy, by a neat deception both frustrates the domineering fathers and simultaneously restores forlorn Jane to her faithful husband. And, very obviously, Simon Eyre assists this unification because his benevolence includes Lacy and Rose; his shop is a center of the action; and his shrewd exuberance wins his acceptance by all of society from King to prentices.

This structural unity is supported by deft transitions of feeling as episode follows episode, without the heavy exploitation of a particular theatrical scene by which Dekker sometimes offends us in other plays. Firke's and Sybil's coarse humor (half of it depending on by-play); the ironic vanity of Margery and the cunning of Simon; moments of pathetic separation and recognition; high hopes of lovers; exultation in successful disguise and deception; suspense for the outcome of a ruse or of the King's intervention; and songs, dances, and crowd scenes—all these are woven by Dekker into supremely good theater.

The realism of *Shoemaker's Holiday*, as I have said, is mainly of a traditional kind, like the romantic elements. It is true, of course, that the earlier popular comedy more often represents the absurdities, including the dialect, of rustic and village types like those in William Stevenson's *Gammer Gurton's Needle* (*circa* 1553), whereas the milieu in *Shoemaker's Holiday* is chiefly that of the city craftsmen. But the transition to London life was a natural one and may even be said to have been anticipated in *George a Greene, the Pinner of Wakefield* (possibly by Robert Greene, 1588), *The Weakest Goeth to the Wall*,[15] and probably in other plays. In *George a Greene* the pugnacious shoemakers of Bedford hob-nob and drink with King Edward; in *The Weakest Goeth to the Wall* a humorous botcher who carries his tools onto the stage (like Eyre's men) figures importantly in the play.

Dekker's own advance upon earlier comic realism appears in only two aspects of *Shoemaker's Holiday*. He paints a single genre picture of the rising of a shopkeeper's household at dawn (I.4), a scene which dwells humorously on the master's futile efforts to get his wife, maids, and benchmen at work before seven. Dekker also shows us, perhaps more believably than ever before, the kind of shrewdness and independence of character, in both Eyre and Sir Roger Otley, which enabled the craftsmen to rise into the merchant class and then to enter the aristocracy. To recall the Dick Whittington legend and Deloney's stories helps to correct any misconception that Dekker was the first to record this breaking of social crust; much rather, we ought simply say that his depiction of it is quite plausible. He was far less interested than Deloney in the maneuvers by which Eyre founded his fortune; and, as for the values which usually motivate such men, if Jonson's and Massinger's plays are compared with *Shoemaker's Holiday,* Dekker reveals no important general truth. Instead, he merely shows us a very likable fellow who profits from a stroke of luck.

To find in *Shoemaker's Holiday* any deep social truth or vision of Elizabethan society is, I think, to see both the play and the society in a sentimental mood. The genuine realism present in the play (beyond that discussed above) is simply the psychological truth which Shakespeare and other masters have trained us to expect in nearly all drama. At times Dekker achieves it. Among such passages is the one[16] where Ralph returns from France to Eyre's shop and weeps from fatigue and grief while callous Mistress Eyre shamefacedly admits that she scolded Jane out of her service (III.2); and almost equally good is the one (IV.3) in which Hammon convinces Jane that Ralph has died in the war. These indeed do have universal appeal and show Dekker at his best. Such poignancy is not found in all scenes of *Shoemaker's Holiday;* but, where it is absent, Dekker is still the master showman and satisfies us with his skillful use of conventions.

IV   *From Romance to Lampoon:* Satiromastix *(1601)*

In Chapter 1 a brief account was given of the War of the Theaters between Ben Jonson and the poetasters (as he described most of the other playwrights) and, in particular, John Marston and Dekker. Doubtless, Jonson labored hard to make *Poetaster* caustic enough to humiliate and frighten into silence all his enemies, including dramatists, actors, and critics. In fact, even today *Poetaster* raises laughter in many scenes and constantly draws admiration for its pungent style. In the days when all its allusions to personalities were clear, it must have been hilariously amusing to the audience at the Blackfriars. But while Jonson was still composing it—a process that took fifteen weeks, as the prologue tells—he learned that his enemies were preparing a counterblast. Jonson's reference to the fact in *Poetaster*, III. 4.352, indicates that he thought Marston was the leader.

However, the play that appeared alternately at the Globe and at the Paul's Boys' theater was *Satiromastix*, a work in which it is very difficult to find traces of Marston's style, but in which Dekker's style and technique are apparent almost everywhere. In the entry in the Stationers' Register and on the title page of the first edition only Dekker's name is mentioned. It is true that the epistle "To the World," which is unsigned but which Dekker certainly wrote, states, "Horace [Jonson] *hal'd his* Poetasters *to the Barre, the* Poetasters *vntruss'd* Horace ..." Yet nine lines below we find, "*I meete one* [critic who blames me] ... *for that in vntrussing* Horace, *I did onely whip his fortunes, and conditions of life, where the more noble* Reprehension *had bin of his mindes* Deformitie...." Throughout the remaining thirty lines of the epistle the pronoun *I* is used in every line, with no mention of Marston. In other collaborations, however, Dekker usually gives credit quite carefully to his partner if there is opportunity to do so. Therefore, it is sensible to conclude that the mention of the untrussing quoted above simply refers to the *action in the play* (V.2.227–232), not to the composition of the play. Professor Bowers has shown that the manuscript which Dekker himself (as it seems) delivered to the publisher was a fair copy of Dekker's earlier draft and was possibly in his own hand, for his spellings are abundant throughout. Moreover, the dramatist read the quarto during or after the printing and furnished an errata list which was issued with the edition. From all this evidence we ought to infer that Marston's contribution to the play can hardly have been more than some general suggestions about the action as well as about the method of lampooning Horace most effectively.

Considering the result of Dekker's effort, Jonson would have been expected to say that Marston probably preferred to let Dekker take full credit. In fact, however, Jonson affected great disdain and withdrew from strife against "bare and beggarly conceits"; and Dekker's epistle "To the World" is written with the gaiety of complete triumph. It is appropriate to analyze those qualities of *Satiromastix* which discouraged Jonson from further combat, as well as those which aroused his contempt.

The main plot, set in the court of King William Rufus near the end of the eleventh century, is a very simple one, a tragic situation that is quickly resolved; it is easily completed in five scenes (I.1, II.1, III.2, V.1, and V.2) of only moderate length in a play that is longer than the average. Sir Walter Terrill, a courtier, marries Cælestine, daughter of Sir Quintilian Shorthose, apparently a rich merchant. The King, who has been invited to the wedding festivity, becomes infatuated with the bride's beauty and dares Sir Walter to show his faith in her purity by sending her to court that night, ostensibly to display her loveliness for a day or so to the nobility. Despite his anguish, Terrill is compelled by pride and honor to swear an oath that he will send her. After the King has gone, the young couple and the father lament this outcome, but Terrill cannot break his word. However, Sir Quintilian finds the ultimate preservative of his daughter's virtue—death by poison. Cælestine drinks the potion and seems to die at once, as Terrill agonizes. That night her body, seated in a chair, is brought by a group of maskers to the King's presence chamber. The King, who has been expecting treacherously to enjoy *droit du seigneur,* unmasks the bride and is aghast to find her dead. When Terrill denounces him as a tyrant, the King repents his evil and acknowledges his guilt. Thereupon, Cælestine revives from the sleeping potion, and the King restores her to Terrill.

It would be unjust to say that the handling of the conflict between love and honor, initiated by the King's dare, typically reveals Dekker's failure as a tragedian. We have too little of his tragedy left us by which to judge. His early tragedies, for which Francis Meres praised him, are lost, and the only surviving later

one, *The Witch of Edmonton,* is a collaboration. But it is true
that Dekker's handling of Terrill's dilemma is characteristic of
his method in romance and tragicomedy. Although *Satiromastix* evolved into a lampoon, the Terrill-Cælestine plot was undoubtedly designed originally as tragicomedy.

Yet the situation consists of very tragic elements: the lovers,
yearning for each other, are tortured by the code of honor which
demands that Terrill manifest his trust in his bride and his King,
thus delaying the consummation of their marriage and, far
worse, threatening to desecrate their love and honor. Dekker
does not falsify or obscure any of these elements; to do so would
have been to frustrate his own intent by robbing his scenes of
full impact. In order to control the audience's response to the
tragic situation, however, he employs two conventions: First, the
play begins and is maintained in the mood of broad comedy, with
the result that the pseudo-tragic situation just escapes being sub-
merged by farce and bawdy humor; second, the familiar device
of a sleeping potion is signalled for the audience by Sir Quintilian's demeanor—he smiles as Terrill weeps over Cælestine's
unconscious body:

> *Terrill.* I had a constant wife, Ile tell the King;
> Vntill the King—what dost thou smile? art thou
> A Father?
> *Sir Quintilian.* Yea, smiles on my cheekes arise,
> To see how sweetly a true virgin dyes.

Before Terrill can protest further, the maskers enter to carry
Cælestine to court. It is notable that the resolution follows at
once; there is no comic interruption. The rapidity of the action
in these climactic scenes must also be credited to Dekker's tact in
handling the theme. It should probably be added that the ceremonies which precede the unmasking of the dead Cælestine con-
tribute to esthetic distancing of the lovers' ordeal and so ob-
viate any tragic pain in the audience's feeling.

The worst charge that criticism can bring against *Satiromastix*
is the painful artificiality of the dialogue among Terrill, Cælestine, and her father as they lament their disastrous situation
(II.1, III.2). Their speeches are woven mostly of empty con-

ceits, silly word-play, commonplace rhetorical patterns and figures; the rhymed couplets are vapid. This inexcusable lapse
in style was probably caused by Dekker's haste and by his shift
of purpose from tragicomedy to satire.

Whether or not we credit Dekker with skill in the management
of the main plot, it is surely plausible to think that he kept that
plot to the brevity and simplicity of its original conception
because of the overgrown comic actions which came to occupy
about four-fifths of the play. Perhaps the comic plot was also
planned more simply at first. It presents the farcical wooing of
foolish Widow Miniver by two suitors: hairy Sir Vaughan ap
Rees, a peppery Welsh knight with a ridiculous dialect, and bald
Sir Adam Prickshaft, whose name contributes much bawdy allusion. Probably in Dekker's first plan a third suitor, a rascally
soldier, rivaled the other two; and he may have been replaced
by Captain Tucca, a boisterous, lewd bully with an amusing vocabulary. Tucca was first introduced by Jonson in *Poetaster;*
Dekker has taken him over with no change except an increase of
his villainy and fantastic scurrility. The rivalry of these three to
win the widow proceeds through absurd trickery and a travesty
of poetic contests to an undeserved success for Tucca.

More amusing than Tucca, however, are three other characters
borrowed from *Poetaster;* Dekker keeps their original identities
but changes the characters to sharpen his ridicule. Horace is
Jonson; Crispinus, Marston; and Demetrius Fannius, Dekker
himself. Naturally, Crispinus and Demetrius emerge fair-minded
moderate men, poets concerned only with defending their repu-
tations from Horace's persistent vilification. Dekker provides
Horace with a moronic admirer, Asinius Bubo, whose historical
identity has not been decided. These pseudo-Roman characters
are intruded into the tragicomedy in several ways: Horace is
employed by Terrill to furnish nuptial songs for the wedding
festivity; Crispinus and Demetrius are included in Terrill's wedding party and have, between them, a total of three short lines
in two scenes (probably the poets have been substituted for
two Norman gentlemen of the court); Horace writes libels, for
pay, against Sir Vaughan ap Rees's rivals and, for malice, bitter
epigrams against Captain Tucca; Sir Vaughan hires Horace to
write an ode in praise of hair, and Sir Adam employs Crispinus

[57]

to recite a versified paradox in praise of baldness—all as strategy in wooing Widow Miniver.

Finally, Horace and Asinius are arraigned before the King in the last scene, as guilty of "... bitter *Satirisme,* of *Arrogance,/* Of *Selfe-loue,* of *Detraction,* of a blacke/And stinking *Insolence.* ..." (V.2.220–222). The satyr suits which the two are wearing are untrussed and pulled off over their heads; then they are crowned with nettles. In *Poetaster,* Jonson provided an excellent satiric climax with the forcing of an emetic on Crispinus to make him vomit up his crudities of poetic diction. Dekker's scene of the untrussing, although less pungent satire, no doubt raised as loud a laughter.

It is not hard to see why Jonson gave up the contest after the production of *Satiromastix.* If the audiences at the private theaters had been polled, they would doubtless have voted *Poetaster* the better play, which it surely is. But Dekker had proved himself quite clever enough to defeat his adversary with the techniques of dramatic caricature—with Jonson's own weapons, in fact. Jonson's aggressive individualism made him a very broad target, and Dekker took full advantage of the fact. Jonson's physique—his red, pockmarked face, thin beard, staring eyes, hollow cheeks, shapeless nose, loud voice, "mountain belly" —are the constant objects of Tucca's malice; and they were probably simulated by the actor playing Horace. Jonson's picturesque history as bricklayer, homicide, jailbird, converted Papist, and itinerant actor dismissed from his company for lack of talent— all are flung at him repeatedly. (We should remember that Jonson's ridicule of Marston's red hair and Dekker's threadbare cloak partly explains and justifies Dekker's venom.) However, more important are Jonson's personality traits shown in action. Horace is exposed as a vain, short-tempered, repetitious, costive rhymester, a railer, a slanderer, a liar, and a coward. His toadyism toward noblemen and his cheating of gull-gallants are admitted even by himself.

Since all these traits had at least a semblance of truth, the remarkable fullness of the portrait must have been relished by many in the audience. Perhaps of equal enjoyment was Dekker's irony in using Jonson's own inventions, especially Horace and Tucca, in drawing the caricature. To relish the irony fully, one would first have to attend *Poetaster* at the Blackfriars and then, a few nights later, *Satiromastix* at Paul's. When Jonson learned that Tucca, whom he had created as a lampoon on an actual boisterous soldier, Captain Hannam, had been turned by Dekker into a lewd abuser of Jonson, he must have seen the futility of any more skirmishes against the poetasters.

Dekker's success in answering caricature with lampoon naturally invites a further comparison of the two plays in terms of their purpose and achievement. In *Poetaster,* Jonson strove for a characteristically high goal and by characteristically high means. We must agree with Professor Talbert that the play "is *primarily* a dramatic defense of poetry." More specifically, it discloses the evils that beset artists, the relations of princes and courtiers to poets, and the high functions of poets in human culture. Its method (not essentially a dramatic one) is "running the gamut of the barbarians," that is, ridiculing successively the various enemies of literary art.[17] Among these, of course, are poetasters; thus, incidentally, Marston and Dekker can be exposed to ridicule. (Doubtless, Jonson elaborated this feature of his plan beyond what strict proportion allowed.) Hence, *Poetaster* stands as an *ars poetica,* a work of literary doctrine, but one adapted for the stage. Its purpose is basically serious; its mode —satire—Jonson was striving with erudition and independence to adapt to theatrical form; its style is witty and eloquent. Despite these impressive claims, *Poetaster* has to be judged by the criterion of vitality in the theater. In this respect it is weaker, for it is thin in plot, though amusing in its episodes; and it is overly long in some speeches and in its totality.

Satiromastix obviously does not have equal merits as literature. A common—and stupid—criticism points out the violation of decorum in putting "Roman" characters into a Medieval story; in reality, Horace is no more a Roman than Sir Quintilian Shorthose is a Norman. Dekker has merely extended the principle used by Jonson in *Poetaster* (and by most other Elizabethan dramatists) of dramatizing contemporary manners and attitudes in an antique setting. If all the names in *Satiromastix* were clearly Norman, nothing in the play would be changed (except to weaken the effect of borrowing from *Poetaster*). Actually to be considered, rather, are the incongruities of tone or dramatic method that vitiate the play. From this point of view we must blame Dekker, in the first place, for the discord between the serious and the comic plots, which seem to be quite devoid of thematic relation to each other. Secondly, Dekker has elaborated the comic theme of Widow Miniver and her suitors to such a degree that the serious action ceases to count much in our imaginations or in the meaning of the play. Thirdly, in the comic plot Dekker has relied too heavily on conventionally crude dialect and farcically shallow characterization.

Yet, without regard to its success as a lampoon of Jonson, Dekker's portrait of Horace must be judged a remarkable comic characterization; and Tucca and Bubo are certainly comparable, if not equal, to Shakespeare's Pistol and Aguecheek. Perhaps no more can be claimed for the farce of Miniver's suitors than that it probably did not bore the audience at Paul's for whom it was written. In other words, like the rest of the play, it is good theater. We have to grant that *Satiromastix* is a potpourri not well blended; yet is not a contemptible work. And it served its original purpose extraordinarily well.

V *Realism Merged with Romantic Convention:*
The Honest Whore *(1604, 1605?)*

Doubtless under the influence of Jonson's *Every Man in His Humour* and *Every Man Out of His Humour,* as well as of Marston's and Middleton's early "city comedies" and the vogue of formal satire from 1597 to 1600, Dekker, in two plays now called *The Honest Whore,*[18] tried to combine realistic depiction of London life with his accustomed morality and romance. Part I is, indeed, a collaboration with Middleton, a realist by temperament. His contribution (unusually limited in number of lines)[19] consists mainly of the shopkeeper scenes, in which the patience, or "humour," of Candido the linendraper is severely tested by his wife and by a crew of idle gallants. Despite the farcical humor of these episodes, Candido's triumphant virtue is eulogized and therefore truly constitutes part of Dekker's morality pattern, which is seen more plainly in the major action: the conversion of Bellafront from whoredom to chastity. Yet, as a dramatist trained in the practices of the early 1590's, Dekker could not let these morality elements compose the whole substance; accordingly, he frames them in a romantic love story. Characteristically, he subordinates realism of social manners to morality, humor, and romance.

The romantic plot has as its basis a familiar situation: the hostility of two noble families imperils the happiness of two lovers, their offspring. Gasparo, Duke of Milan, seeks to terminate the love affair of his daughter Infelice with Hippolito (whose family is not named); he arranges to have Dr. Benedict give the girl a sleeping potion; when it takes effect, the Duke announces that his daughter has died. After a public funeral procession which is interrupted by Hippolito's frantic demand for possession of the body and by his accusation of murder against the Duke, Infelice awakens in her bed chamber and is told that Hippolito is dead. She is taken to Bergamo for seclusion. The Duke now suggests to his accomplice that Hippolito should be poisoned; but although he seems to consent promptly (I.3.99), Dr. Benedict secretly initiates the moves that will frustrate the Duke by communicating the truth to the lovers, first, by a letter to Infelice and, secondly, by a talk with Hippolito.

The audience, however, cannot immediately see this apparent reversal of Dr. Benedict's character because three acts of the play intervene before his communications are made (IV.4). Meanwhile, the romance is suspended, and the other plots occupy the stage. When, at last, Hippolito learns from Dr. Benedict that Infelice is alive, the romance moves swiftly to its end. Aided by the physician, the lovers meet at Bethlehem Monastery, seven miles from Milan, where Friar Anselmo agrees to marry them in the evening; afterwards, they may escape under cover of darkness. But the gabbling tongue of Matheo, Hippolito's friend, has already given news of the plan to a courtier, who, in turn, has told it to the Duke. Another of Hippolito's friends brings word of the Duke's pursuit. The wedding is quickly performed. Although Bellafront does prevent the lovers from escaping in disguise as friars and does expose them, the Duke soon resigns himself to the marriage, for he has had no antipathy to Hippolito as a man.

The morality plot is more important than the romance, both in its very essence and in the amount of action given to it. Matheo, a dissolute gallant, has taken as his mistress the courtesan

Bellafront; but she falls in love with Hippolito when Matheo brings his friend for a casual visit. Later, she privately avows her love to Hippolito, expecting his ready acquiescence in her passion; Hippolito, instead, replies with a lengthy diatribe about the odious character and fate of a whore. After he has gone, Bellafront is overcome with shame and love. She prepares to kill herself with the dagger which Hippolito accidentally left behind. But he returns for the weapon and prevents her suicide.

Repenting her evil life, Bellafront discharges her bawd and pimp and then rebuffs the group of gallants who frequent her lodging. However, her plea to Matheo that he marry her and restore her honor (he was her original seducer) is in vain. Although her renewed plea for Hippolito's love is equally fruitless, still her visit to his apartment enables her to overhear his appointment to meet Dr. Benedict. By some means, presumably from Matheo, Bellafront learns of the rendezvous at Bethlehem. There, after gaining entrance as a mad woman, she finds the Duke in a pliant mood and appeals to him for justice against Matheo. The Duke orders the wastrel to marry her, and the betrothal takes place as part of the play's resolution.

The comic plot exhibits the patience of the merchant Candido. The efforts of Viola, his perverse wife, to vex him seem to have no motive other than a sense of inferiority brought on by his self-control. Her envy is seconded by the mischief of a group of idle gallants. The action is dispersed throughout the play, mostly in Acts I, III, and IV, and consists of a series of tricks played on the imperturbable, but not stupid, merchant. Finally, soon after Viola has had him carried off to Bethlehem as a madman, she repents this trick and her envy. The Duke's sudden journey to the monastery causes her to follow in order to obtain Candido's release.

From these summaries it is apparent that the structure of Part I is less unified than that of *The Shoemaker's Holiday*. Two rather mechanical devices serve to tie the three actions together. The first of these is Hippolito's friendship with Matheo, which has no foundation in the men's qualities but is invented for economy: to allow Hippolito to function in both romantic and morality plots. Of course, this same function is performed by the group of gallants who serve as tormentors of

Candido in the comic plot and as companions (in fact, one of them acts as informant) of the Duke in the love plot. The second device is Dekker's gathering of all the characters at Bethlehem Monastery, which, rather surprisingly, also houses Bedlam Hospital. Setting the denouement in Bedlam permits Dekker to entertain his audience with a show of madmen, which has but little relation to his drama. The gathering itself, however, once the lovers have circumvented the hostile father, facilitates the resolution. The Duke, in a rather sketchy judicial scene, deals out rewards to Bellafront and Candido.

Viewed as a structural device, Dr. Benedict's duplicity in his relations with Duke Gasparo is a little less mechanical. Benedict at first seems the ordinary tool-villain of Italianate melodrama (I.3); later scenes, however, lead to a different interpretation. We discover that he has always been the friend of the lovers; his offer to poison Hippolito (I.3.96–97) is only a ruse by which he may meet the young man, conceal him, and bring about the wedding. Far from acting the villain or the pretentious quack (conventional object of satire), Benedict functions like the kindly friar in other romantic comedies, especially Lawrence (in *Romeo and Juliet*) who is also learned in physic. In Act I, Benedict indicates by intonation and facial expression his secret horror of Gasparo's command to poison Hippolito; we note "although the fact ['deed'] be fowle" (I.3.99). Even before falsely reporting Hippolito's death to Gasparo, Benedict has written the whole truth to Infelice and summoned her to Bethlehem to meet her lover (IV.4.94–97). His long delay in revealing the truth to Hippolito has resulted from being "chambred vp,/To stop discouery" (IV.4.82–83). His false report to the Duke of Hippolito's death has no plot function other than to revive the tension which has grown weak because of two and one-half acts devoted to the morality and comic actions. Gasparo is thus again shown to be a treacherous tyrant.

In summary, the audience's interpretation of the Physician's function in the play depends on the actor's skill in revealing his duplicity by conventional inflections, looks, and gestures more than on symbolism of costume or on the pattern of action, although the pattern is discernible after Benedict's introductory scene. After he has informed Hippolito of the plan for the secret wedding, Dr. Benedict disappears from the play. Friar Anselmo substitutes for him in Act V, and perhaps the same actor played both parts.

Although the artificiality of the plot devices used by Dekker in this play would be far less noticeable in the theater than it is to a reader, the dramatist is undeniably less skillful than in *The Shoemaker's Holiday* in applying technique to his purposes, particularly in the device of Hippolito's and Matheo's friendship. This tie seems especially implausible because the moral worlds of the romance and the morality plots are not assimilated (Part II is much better unified in this respect). Furthermore, if we take realism to mean the dramatist's representation of the drives and tensions of normal life and not just fidelity to language and social manners, we must say about Part I of *The Honest Whore*, as about *Shoemaker's Holiday*, that Dekker has subordinated realism to other purposes. When we look, for instance, at the only episode (II.1) which achieves notable satiric force—the scene where Bellafront makes her toilet and then entertains the gallants—we admire the vivid depiction in the first 230 lines and then its sequel—Hippolito's eloquent invective against whoredom. Jonson could not have improved either part. Underlying the whole scene, however, is a double motif that Jonson would have avoided: Bellafront instantaneously falls in love with Hippolito and, as a result of this emotional impetus, is changed at once from a frivolous, coarsened woman to a repentant sinner. Dekker's keen observation and brilliant style become the vehicles of familiar conventions of romance.

Although the scene displays great mastery of dramatic effects and truth to human feeling, at the end of it, beyond question, carnal love really dominates Bellafront: "Not speake to me! not looke! not bid farewell!/Hated! this must not be, some meanes Ile try./Would all Whores were as honest now, as I" (II.1.454–456). Therefore, we have to deny Dekker credit for the deepest ethical feeling or psychological intuition. The same confusion of motives holds in Bellafront's remaining scenes and is even accentuated by less satisfactory theatrical conventions: the disguise of a page boy, the pretended madness, and the hackneyed recovery of Bellafront's virtue by a forced marriage to Matheo, her first seducer. She must be married, for this is a comedy.[20]

In spite of these reservations about the limited realism of Part I, the play is impressive for its scenes of pathos and poetry. Not much below Dekker's finest work, it apparently succeeded well on stage and was printed in four editions before 1616.

There is unanimity that Part II of *The Honest Whore* is wholly Dekker's, and the very general opinion is that this play is one of his best. Naturally seeking to repeat a successful formula, he offers the same principal characters—Bellafront, Hippolito, Matheo, and Infelice—as well as another testing of Candido, a fifth act enlivened by the humors of Bridewell (instead of Bedlam), and a reversal of the original moral situation. The reversal is the one to which Somerset Maugham devotes ponderous irony in *Rain*: the converted courtesan is pursued by the man who has won her back to virtue. But Dekker, never a cynic, has too deep a faith in human nature for an ironic ending. He is intent now on a domestic comedy (rather than a romantic one); but it must be moral. The action, however, is not simple but quite complicated.

After Matheo has been imprisoned for killing his opponent in a duel, Bellafront comes to Hippolito who is now happily married to Infelice. She brings Matheo's plea for help in getting a pardon. Hippolito, who promises to intercede with Duke Gasparo, is captivated by Bellafront's beauty. Later he meets her father, Orlando Friscobaldo, who has tried to cast her off and forget her because of her disgraceful life. Although Friscobaldo tells Hippolito that he will not help Bellafront, afterwards, disguised as a servant, he goes to Matheo's house. He arrives just after Matheo, released from jail by Hippolito's intervention, has been joyfully welcomed by Bellafront. She pleads with her husband to amend his life, but he is eager to return to his cronies. Friscobaldo, who offers to become Matheo's servant, is hired under the name of Pacheco.

Hippolito has tried to corrupt Bellafront's virtue with gifts; in particular, he bribes Pacheco to give her a purse full of gold. But Bellafront returns all the gifts to Hippolito through Friscobaldo. When Friscobaldo comes to Hippolito's house and delivers the gifts to Infelice, he thereby reveals that her husband is pursuing Bellafront. Later, Infelice cleverly draws from Hippolito a confession of his intended adultery. Ignoring his remorse, she indignantly denounces him. In his resentment he resolves to continue to woo Bellafront.

Matheo has meanwhile gambled away every penny he owns, even his sword and cloak. He comes home and urges Bellafront to go into the streets to sell her body. She refuses, and Matheo strips off her gown and sends Friscobaldo to pawn it, leaving Bellafront standing in her petticoat. When Matheo's friend, the courtier Lodovico, visits them, he gives Matheo one of his own suits. Friscobaldo's indignation has reached such a pitch that he goes home, puts on his own garments, and returns to Matheo's place as his father to berate the couple, especially Matheo. In Lodovico's fine clothing, Matheo has the effrontery to return Friscobaldo equal abuse. The father refuses to lend them money, leaves Matheo's house, resumes his servant's dress, and returns as Pacheco.

Matheo now tells him of a plan to rob old Friscobaldo. Left alone, Bellafront receives a visit from Hippolito, and the two engage in a formal argument on whoredom. Bellafront ends it by running away, but Hippolito continues in his determination to win her.

Friscobaldo reveals his identity to Duke Gasparo as well as a plan for arresting Matheo for robbery. The Duke supplements this plot by ordering the arrest of all prostitutes in Milan and their confinement in Bridewell. By this means he hopes to shame Hippolito out of his attachment to Bellafront. At a gathering of gallants and panders in Matheo's house (to which the innocent merchant Candido has also been invited), sergeants of the law arrest Matheo, Bellafront, Candido, and the panders and take them all to Bridewell. When the Duke, Infelice, Hippolito, and their retinue pay a visit to Bridewell, Bellafront pleads with the Duke for Matheo's pardon. Matheo admits to the robbery of Friscobaldo, but charges his wife with being both his accomplice and the whore of Hippolito. Infelice corroborates the second accusation. Hippolito furiously proclaims Bellafront's purity. At this point Pacheco-Friscobaldo removes his disguise. Matheo and Hippolito are overwhelmed with shame and confess their guilt. At Bellafront's renewed plea, Friscobaldo and the Duke pardon Matheo. Friscobaldo takes Matheo and Bellafront to live in his own house. Hippolito and Infelice are reconciled.

At the beginning of the minor plot we learn that the patient linen-draper, Candido, has lost his first wife and has just married for a second time. When his bride displays her temper at the wedding feast, the gallants, led by Lodovico, propose to teach Candido how to discipline a new wife. Disguised as a prentice, Lodovico induces Candido and his wife to duel with yardsticks; but she quickly submits to her husband. Thereafter, two other gullings of Candido follow; the second involves Candido's arrest for receiving stolen goods, a disgrace which he endures with patience and from which he is exonerated in Bridewell. The comic scenes are less ironically amusing than those in Part I.

Although Part II is crammed with intrigue, it is much more highly unified in theme than Part I. Part II is a successful blend of motifs from saints' legends and from Prodigal Son interludes of the earlier sixteenth century. Professor Michael Manheim's illuminating article on the themes of this play (see note 18 above) gives a persuasive demonstration of Dekker's artistry in the blending of all the elements of the work, including both the rather obscure one in which Hippolito dismisses the poor scholar (I.1) and the Bridewell scenes (V.2). Bellafront must resist Hippolito's seduction, patiently endure Matheo's cruelty, and strive to win him to an honest life by her devotion. Her ordeal is, in considerable part, a new version of the legend of Thais who, following her conversion from a life of lustfulness to one of purity, has to endure a severe test of her virtue.

Bellafront's tempter, Hippolito, parallels other representatives of the Prodigal Son in several plays of about the year 1600— Young Flowerdale, for example, in the anonymous *London Prodigal* (published 1605). However, Dekker has greatly modified the character-type by making Hippolito older and happily married; and his reform is not accomplished by the intervention of his own disguised father. Furthermore, there are no palliating circumstances for his lust. He is tested, and his vice is exposed, first by Infelice, then more decisively by Friscobaldo, who thereby reforms him. In fact, Friscobaldo is the agent, the disguised father, who puts Bellafront, Matheo, and Hippolito

[67]

to the test and thereby both glorifies Bellafront's fortitude and reveals the corruption of the two men.

Purity and fortitude against temptation are not the same virtue as patience, which Bellafront also possesses to the highest degree, and which is Candido's strength. Bellafront is reminiscent, therefore, of Griselda as well as of Thais. In respect to patience, the other wronged wife, Infelice,[21] becomes a foil to Bellafront by her lack of sufferance. When, by a clever ruse, she has led Hippolito to confess his infidelity, her wrath simply provokes an answering anger in him and a fresh resolve to possess Bellafront. Thus Infelice's impatience is punished.

The moral lesson receives even more enforcement, however. The Candido plot, in two actions, dramatizes, first, the shopkeeper's very quick taming of his shrew, his new wife, who kneels and says submissively, " ... I disdaine/The wife that is her husbands Soueraigne" (II.2.108–109). Secondly, his sublime patience is demonstrated in Bridewell through the trickery of the gallants. A medieval expression of the moral lesson of the Thais theme is a formal debate of over 130 lines (IV.1.256–394) between Bellafront and Hippolito on whoredom. Professor Manheim points out that this highly rhetorical argument is a reversal of the positions of the two contestants in Part I and gives the rhetorical victory to the woman. In Part I, Bellafront, in lustful passion, spoke the sophistries which truth, in Hippolito's person, refuted with indignant sincerity. In Part II, Hippolito, appealing directly to the audience for a verdict, states his case first and plays the role of lustful Fallacy; then Truth movingly confutes him.

Bellafront's virtue conquers at last, but does not triumph directly over Matheo's vice. As in life, virtue triumphs by drawing on the aid of friends—her father and the Duke. Friscobaldo's intrigue finally brings Matheo to shame and repentance.[22] By testing Bellafront's firmness, then, Friscobaldo plays a more important part in the dramatization of the theme than at first appears. Hazlitt and others have fervently praised the character of Friscobaldo as one of Dekker's best creations. Undoubtedly he is, but readers who are inclined to unsparing realism may consider the execrable Matheo a finer masterpiece of truth. After he has lost hat, cloak, and rapier at dice, Matheo returns home and tries to drive Bellafront into the streets to sell herself: "Must haue money, must haue some, must haue a Cloake, and Rapier, and things: will you goe set your limetwigs, and get me some birds, some money?... Must haue cash and pictures: doe ye heare, (frailty)?" (III.2.27–32). But when she refuses to go, Matheo begins to strip off her clothing in order to pawn it.

Unable to endure his daughter's degradation, Friscobaldo removes his disguise as servant, enters in his own person, and vilifies Matheo as a thief, cheater, and whoremonger, only to hear himself labeled an ass, churl, and mangy mule. In the course of this abusive exchange, Matheo asides to Bellafront: "Kneele, and get money of him.... Hang upon him ... follow close ... to him" (IV.1.120, 123–124). A little later, however, and strangely, Matheo's pride causes him to choke on learning that the roast of mutton he is relishing was given by a charitable neighbor! Scenes III.2 and IV.1 are genre pictures of sordid life unequalled in Elizabethan drama, not excepting Shakespeare's. The whole play shows signs of great care on Dekker's part. We can only wish he had sacrificed some of the didactic theatricalism of the Bridewell scenes for more of Matheo in action.

VI *Patriotic Allegory:* The Whore of Babylon *(1606)*

In publishing *The Whore of Babylon* in 1607, Dekker was clearly offering his politico-religious allegory with pride and confidence to his countrymen.[23] Although the theme of the play is the preservation of Elizabeth from assassination and of England from the Armada—events which had taken place more than nineteen years before—Dekker does not refer to any anachronism in the subject-matter for two probable reasons: His devotion to Elizabeth had not changed since his youth, and he was confident that the intense national emotion consequent on the discovery of the Gunpowder Plot was like his own and would applaud his patriotic poem. With respect to the Spenserian theme of England's destiny, Dekker is offering in drama a counterpart to *The Faerie Queene.* The opening sentence of *Lectori* has an obvious Spenserian phrasing: "The Generall scope of this Drammatical Poem, is to set forth (in Tropicall and shadowed collours) the Greatnes, Magnanimity, Constancy, Clemency, and the other incomparable Heroical vertues of our late Queene."

To be precise, the play is a political and religious allegory of England's former escape from peril, a figuring forth of the malignancy of England's secular enemies, Spain and Catholicism. For several reasons the Gunpowder Plot itself would not serve as a basis for a poem: its circumstances were too confused, and James I was not entirely English! But, from a perspective of seventeen years (to the time of the Plot), a Protestant Englishman could see infallibly the hand of Providence in the course of events in the 1580's. Dekker had probably long meditated on the dramatization of the theme. Spenser was above challenge in the epic, but a worthy poetic drama on England's greatest trial had never appeared.

Neither Dekker's aspiration nor its result is ridiculous. In 1606 the majority of Londoners, if not of all Englishmen, must have shared his belief that God had again intervened directly to save England; he quite truly expressed their feelings about the dangers from Spain and Catholicism. Eighteen years later the failure of the negotiations for the marriage of Prince Charles to the Infanta provoked an outburst of the same feeling and force; and Middleton, borrowing here and there from Dekker's play, wrote for the King's Men one of the most successful political satires ever staged in England, *A Game at Chesse* (1624). Both the parallels and the contrasts between the two plays are interesting. We note in particular that Middleton boldly ventures to represent the events of recent months in Spain; Dekker's reference to the Gunpowder Plot is only by implication. His choice of the Armada-peril for his theme may have been a mistake because of the distance in time and the lack of correspondence of details with the events of the Plot. Whatever the reason, there is no record of any notable success for *The Whore of Babylon*. Dekker, perhaps rationalizing, complains of the "bad handling" which the Prince's Men gave his play at the Fortune Theater.[24]

In summary, the action of the play appears disjointed because the theme is exemplified in two dramatic modes: a pageant-like series of events which were rather remotely connected, historically and chronologically, and a number of interspersed imaginary and allegorical episodes. After a dumb show has represented the death of Queen Mary, the accession of Titania (Elizabeth), and the conversion of Fairie Land (England) to true religion, the

Empress of Babylon (the Roman Church) incites her sons, the hierarchy, to send priests for the purpose of causing confusion in England. Moreover, the monarchs of Spain, France, and the Holy Roman Empire come to Fairie Land to propose marriage with Titania. She refuses them and jeers at their indignation.

Threatening vengeance, the King of France and the Emperor depart, but Satyrane, the King of Spain, stays in the hope of spreading poisonous doctrine, "suck[ing] allegiance from the common breast." Titania's wise counselors prepare for both insurrection within and invasion from without. Danger from within takes the form of two ambitious men, Paridel (Dr. Parry) and Campeius (Edmund Campion). But their malice meets with clemency, not death, from the Queen; they are banished. Appropriately, the Hollanders and the Prince of Portugal come to her for protection and receive it.

At a great council in Babylon (Spain), the Empress, the King of France, and the Emperor determine to assassinate Titania. For this purpose they employ Campeius and Dr. Ropus (Lopez), who have been seduced from their loyalty to Fairie Land by the King of Spain. The two renegades are sent to Fairie Land. Meantime, the council members agree to make an irresistible attack with Spain's immense sea power. Paridel, who has come under the sway of the Jesuits in Rome, is also despatched to Fairie Land.

Titania is unwillingly forced to condemn Mary, Queen of Scots, to death; but by words alone she overawes a lesser enemy, an assassin, and he flees from her unguarded presence. Dr. Ropus's poison plot and Paridell's dealing with Babylon are discovered, but Titania takes no vengeance. Meanwhile, the Armada has been launched from Babylon. When Paridel decides to kill the Queen one of his kinsmen reveals the plan to her courtiers, and before Paridel can muster courage to slay her, even though she is alone, he is apprehended.

Titania and her advisers make preparations for defense against the Armada. However, we learn of the disastrous defeat from the anguished cries of the three kings who witness it from afar (they are on stage). Titania is with her army in camp at Tilbury where Florimell (the Earl of Leicester) brings her news of the victory. Meanwhile, in Babylon, the Empress, hearing of the disaster, rages against the kings. The Emperor defies her, but France and Spain submit to her tyranny. Thus it ends.

The allegorical figures in *The Whore of Babylon* are Time (the father of Truth), Truth, Falsehood, and Plain Dealing. In addition to the initial dumbshow mentioned above, there are three others. In one we see the King of Spain's frustrated attempt to cast a fatal spell on Titania. In another the Empress of Babylon shows her satanic pride as she rides the seven-headed beast. In the last dumbshow Falsehood tries to penetrate Fairie Land with her crew of priests and traitors, such as Edmund Campion. Falsehood's disguise as Truth is exposed, and during this disclosure we learn that Plain Dealing has formerly (in the Middle Ages) mistaken Falsehood for Truth and has been her follower. Enlightened now, Plain Dealing follows Time and Truth as they pursue Falsehood with intent to denounce her. By this allegory Dekker wishes to transfer the medieval peasant, as spokesman of complaint or satire against social evils, into the contemporary world of Protestant England. Accordingly, Plain Dealing's most important dramatic function is to inform Titania of abuses which she is unable to observe because of her protected position—for instance, corruption among the clergy. The only characteristic element of comedy in this play appears in the contrast between Plain Dealing's blunt manner and Titania's gracious, serious bearing and language.

Dekker's intention—to manifest God's providential care for England and true religion through the creation and defense of Queen Elizabeth—is, of course, one of instruction. If that thesis and nothing more were demonstrated, the result might be simply reassurance or complacency for the audience. Although the play does not preach the moral conclusion, Dekker certainly intended that this moral be drawn: kings, lords, and commons, all alike, must hold God's favor by reforming abuses in the commonwealth and seeking justice and other virtues in Church and State. This theme is also present in one of his plague pamphlets which will be discussed in a later chapter.

Because the total import of the play is of such gravity, the dramatist was required to find the most direct, the clearest, and the most meaningful mode of instruction known to him. Dekker accordingly turned back to the traditional genres of the chronicle play and the interlude, each recognized as charged with meaning, the one with patriotism, the other with moral truth. In post-Reformation days the genres had even been combined, as in the plays of John Bale and Sir David Lindsay. But there were no recent Elizabethan examples of such fusion for Dekker to imitate, and we should allow him the measure of originality he claims in his Prologue, that his "Muse/ (Thats thus inspir'de) a Nouell path does tread. . . ." (22–23). Ignoring the "thin vailes" of poetic fiction which cover the identities of persons, we find that essentially *The Whore of Babylon* presents history with the freedom and forthright moral purpose of the chronicle-interlude.

The fiction, however, is an important component of the work, for it controls the tone of the play. Although Dekker does not use the term "allegory," his expression "Tropicall and shadowed collours" reveals his conception of his "Drammaticall Poem" (*Lectori*, 1–2). Transparent as the veil of the fiction was meant to be, the allegory makes more appropriate Dekker's use of such familiar medieval devices as long speeches of narrative and doctrine, groups of generalized characters to represent powers and forces (cardinals, kings, priests, and soldiers), and personified abstractions (Time, Truth, Plain Dealing). Although dumb-shows were largely of Italian Renaissance origin, they and such theatrical spectacles as processions and councils were also appropriate to allegorical plays; and they have their counterparts in literary allegory from *Piers Plowman* to *The Faerie Queene*. Of course, Dekker actually borrows some details from Spenser's poem and attempts by doing so to increase the grandeur of his theme and style, to make his drama and Spenser's epic twin triumphs of English poetry and patriotism.

Among the borrowings are these: England imaged as a fairy land; the gathering of the knights at Titania's court; the frustrating of a conjuror's attempted enchantment of the Queen; Falsehood masquerading as Truth; and the names "Paridel" and "Satyrane," though the persons have nothing in common with Spenser's. (Incidentally, Dekker uses no archaism of language.) But the pervasive influence of Spenser is shown in Dekker's endeavor to idealize both Elizabeth's character and the glories of England in her reign. Undoubtedly his attitude was common; we find the philosophical courtier, Fulke Greville, expressing it in his life of Sir Philip Sidney (*circa* 1610). Therefore, Dekker was not naïve in his feeling, whatever may be our judgment of his accomplishment in *The Whore of Babylon*.

Despite the timely patriotic fervor of *The Whore of Babylon* and its eloquent verse, the audience may have found its dramaturgy too old-fashioned. Tastes in drama were changing, and the causes of change probably lay in both social and literary movements. Among the latter were the vogue of formal satire in verse and of melancholy in society and in literature, the revival of revenge tragedy and of character-writing, and especially the trend toward satiric realism which Jonson's experimental comedies had launched in English drama. Whatever the relative importance of these developments, they either corresponded to or caused changes which we can observe, around 1600, in the plays written for the public theaters by such dramatists as Thomas Heywood, John Webster, Shakespeare, and Dekker himself. A tendency was growing toward social realism, toward Italianate tragedy, and toward romance dominated either by tragic feeling or by deeper psychological interest than had prevailed before. Accompanying a sharpened concentration on human personality was a gradual abandonment of didacticism by means of personified abstractions, overt conflict of good with evil, and loose, episodic structure, as in *Old Fortunatus*. True, we must guard against exaggerating the rapidity of the change, for the era of the clown, the dumbshow, and the generalized character extended well beyond 1600, as Shakespeare's *Cymbeline* reminds us. However, the theme, and especially the technique, of *The Whore of Babylon* must have appeared somewhat archaic to the audience at the Fortune.

In addition, a degree of ambiguity in the play's appeal may have helped to dampen the audience's response. At least to a twentieth-century reader, the alternation of two feelings—indignation against the venality, ambition, and disloyalty of wretches like Campion and Parry along with contempt for their baseness —makes a rather incoherent emotional pattern. Furthermore, since the virtue of Titania and her counselors and warriors is unconquerable when supported by Heaven's favor, then fear of Babylon is superfluous.

[*74*]

To reason in this way, however, leads us to ignore the anxiety created by the Gunpowder Plot, a fear for which the play is meant as an antidote; and we overlook the exultation generated by victory over the plotters and the renewed interest in the subject of political assassination. It should be noted also that *The Whore of Babylon*, through Plain Dealing's words, attacks evils in contemporary England: vices rampant in London; indolence among the clergy; licentious satire in drama; avarice among lawyers; and graft in the army. Hence, although the play capitalizes to a degree on the public's emotion at the moment, the dramatist does not fail to indicate the serious lessons to be drawn from his picture of England protected by divine intervention.

Certainly the poor reception of the play cannot be charged to any lack of attention on Dekker's part. He has surely used the techniques of earlier Elizabethan drama with as much skill as Thomas Kyd or Robert Greene could have shown at their best. And he has evidently devoted great care to the eloquent verse; in fact, nothing that he has left us is better than many of the poetic passages in *The Whore of Babylon*. The Empress of Babylon begins an address to her Council:

> When those Cælestial bodies that doe moue,
> Within the sacred Spheres of Princes bosomes
> Goe out of order, tis as if yon Regiment,
> Weare all in vp-roare; heauen should then be vext,
> Me thinkes such indignation should resemble,
> Dreadfull eclypses, that portend dire plagues
> To nations, fall to Empires, death to Kings,
> To Citties deuastation, to the world,
> That vniuersall hot calamitie
> Of the last horror. (III.1.3–12)

(It seems that the young Milton may have included this play in his reading.)

Again, in Act V, Scene 2, Florimel describes the preparations against the Armada in a style that may be compared with familiar passages in Shakespeare's *Henry V:*

> Your goodly ships beare the most royall freight,
> That the world owes (true hearts:) their wombes are ful,
> Of noble spirits, each man in his face

Shewes a Kings daunting looke, the souldiers stand
So thickly on the decke, so brauely plum'd,
 (The Silken streamers wauing or'e their heades)
That (seeing them) you would judge twere *Pentecost*
And that the iollie youngsters of your townes,
Had flockt togither in gay multitudes,
For May-games, and for summer merriments,
They looke so cheerely: In such little roome
So many Faieries neuer dwelt at once,
Neuer so many men were borne so soone.... (168–180)

VII   *Social Satire:* If This Be Not a Good Play,
the Devil Is in It *(1610?)*

I have noted in Chapter 1 that an interval of about four years, apparently devoted to writing tracts, falls between 1606 and 1610, when, to judge by topical allusions in it, Dekker composed *If This Be Not a Good Play*.[25] After it had been rejected by the Prince's Men at the Fortune, the play was performed by the Queen's Men (formerly the Earl of Worcester's Men, to whom Henslowe gave financial aid). It played at the Red Bull where, traditionally, popular drama prevailed. The refusal by the Prince's company, probably served to complete Dekker's embitterment which began with what he felt was that company's failure with *The Whore of Babylon*.

However, the old-fashioned theme and manner of the play perhaps explain the rejection by the Prince's Men. Discarding altogether the technique developed by Jonson and Middleton for depicting life and manners with pungent realism, Dekker employs a folk tale not merely for explicit moral purposes, but very much in the fashion of a moral interlude of a half-century before; and once again he calls on the traditional stage conventions and devices for spectacle.

The Danish and German tale of Friar Ruus (or Rausch) had been available in English since 1568, but in a form crudely altered from the primitive version. However, as C. H. Herford observes, Dekker returned "by sheer dramatic instinct to the original legend, in the face of every version of it which he can possibly have known."[26] That is to say, Dekker rejected the picture of a corrupt monastery and restored the orderly house described in the

[76]

primitive form of the legend in order to provide a greater challenge to the devil. In fact, although the friars are the object of much of the comedy, their superior, Clement, is a saint; the worst among them can be charged only with stupidity and callousness; and the portrayal of monasticism is free of the contemptuous malice that usually inspires such Elizabethan references to convents as those in the anonymous play *The Merry Devil of Edmonton* and in Middleton's *A Game at Chesse*. Compared to financier Bartervile, the friars in *If This Be Not a Good Play* appear virtuous.

Stated more precisely, Dekker's plan is to show three spheres of human life beset by the power of evil: the court; the Church; and the merchant class. Dekker intends a satire on contemporary life and if his view is not so wide as Jonathan Swift's, it is surely broad enough for a play. It is somewhat medieval in its method. After a superb first scene which presents a conclave in Hell, Satan despatches three devils, one to King Alphonso's court, a second to the priory, and a third to a financier. The success of these three tempters, of course, provides the fundamental satiric comment. At court, Bohor destroys Alphonso's idealism with no loss of time and with little trouble; in the priory, Rush has but limited success and corrupts only a few friars (the play reveals that religion suffers far more from men than from devils); but, in the counting house, Lurchall is at first overmatched by the ingenuity and unscrupulousness of a Machiavellian atheist who believes only in "nature." At the end Lurchall manages to trick the merchant into damnation. Because Dekker intends this drama to be a comedy, in the medieval as well as in the Elizabethan sense, its result must not be cynicism or utter pessimism. Corrupt King Alphonso is saved, therefore, by the humility, constancy, and love of his betrothed wife Ermenhild (still another patient Griselda); and the friary is preserved from destruction by Clement's courage and fortitude.[27]

Two great evils of contemporary England have been illustrated for a courtly or a general audience: the power of greedy counselors at court and the ruthless avarice among the merchant class. But the monarch (in the person of King Alphonso) has also been reproached. Instead of serving as the fountainhead of justice, he has protected the monopolists and has neglected soldiers, scholars, and sailors, the defenders of civilization. The nation may readily take a lesson from Dekker's moral poem, for so he regards it.[28]

Surely no play in the canon is more characteristic of Dekker's mind than this one. As Herford says:

With no other help than his sound playwright's instincts, and without a suspicion of its immense potentialities, he had stumbled upon the very idea afterwards carried out in Goethe's *Faust*—the recasting of an old devil-story in terms of modern society. . . . Unhappily, however, Decker was, after all, little more than a hack with ideas.[29]

Herford's conclusion, however, is quite unfair, whatever defects of art *If This Be Not a Good Play* possesses, for Dekker, could scarcely think otherwise than as a man of the sixteenth century. He was as incapable of Machiavelli's cynicism (in *Belphegor*) as of Goethe's egoism; for, as a Christian, he had to look at society as one who believes in sin, individual responsibility, and grace. In the tracts which he had been writing before *If This Be Not a Good Play*—such as *The Seven Deadly Sins of London, A Knight's Conjuring,* and *Work for Armorers*—he had exposed and satirized social evils of many kinds; and that concentration had been preparation for the play. Whereas our own tendency in this century has been to criticize Dekker for his blindness to society's responsibility for these evils, our more recent emphasis on the need for commitment now makes Dekker's attitude more acceptable.

The epilogue of this play (incorporated as V.4) may be regarded as an adequate summation of Dekker's view of the corruption in English society and, substantially, in all human society. When Dekker gives us his version of the *Inferno,* the walls of Hell open up. Seen in the flames are, first, Guy Faux and Ravaillac, traitors to their kings and countries, and themselves victims of Catholicism's malignancy; next appears a prodigal, a typical courtier who in one year "spent on whores, fooles and slaues,/ An Armies maintenance"; then an extortionate merchant; finally, a Puritan, a black, shrunken soul, the betrayer of the English Church, the raiser of such a hellish uproar that Satan cannot make himself heard. Treason, waste, cruelty, and heresy are the cardinal sins. They are four, not seven; and the emphasis on treason as the most heinous shows a disappointing Elizabethan bias. Nevertheless, the scene and the whole play are rooted in medieval philosophy handed down through morality play, homily, and satire.

Compared with *Old Fortunatus,* Dekker's *If This Be Not a Good Play* would be difficult to revive today in the spirit in which it was written, not because it is more serious than his *Old Fortunatus,* but because its fundamental dramatic irony is a mode from which Dekker could never draw a flow of witty humor. A hasty reader may say that Dekker's use of the Belphegor theme degenerates into platitude or that its irony is lost in mere spectacle. Although unfair, that judgment would have some truth in it. Perhaps the only notable success of Dekker's irony is Lurchall's first frustration in handling Bartervile, the Machiavellian usurer. Dekker lacked the capacity to sustain the tone of that encounter, yet he had chosen a theme which required a strong gift for irony. To his credit, he refrained from supplying,[30] in place of ironic wit, buffoonery by Rush among the friars, as his source and as Christopher Marlowe's *Doctor Faustus* had prompted him to do. Even Scumbroth, the comic cook, is a restrained example of Dekker's usual clown. However, an unresolved tension between the expectations raised by the ironic situation and by Dekker's failure to satisfy them is the weakness of the play. The characters of devils impersonating men create but little satiric humor. At times the essential irony seems almost forgotten.

VIII   *The Fletcherian Influence:*
Match Me in London *(1620?)*

Although chronology has been of merely general relevance in our discussion thus far, the plays (except *Old Fortunatus*) have been considered in the order of their composition; and we have now arrived at about the year 1611. *Match Me in London,* the drama to which I now turn, was probably written between 1620 and 1623 soon after Dekker's release from debtors' prison.[31] This work also represents, no doubt, a number of lost plays composed during the period from 1610 to 1620 during which John Fletcher's prestige was growing in the London theaters. It is also true that out of approximately six surviving plays ascribed to Dekker and written after 1619, only *Match Me in London* is his alone, as the title page and the dedication reveal. Although some of the collaborations are better dramas, the inclusion of *Match Me in London* in this account is justified because it reveals Dekker's individual accommodation to the prevailing tendency in later Stuart drama.

Considering the variety of the plays that may reliably be attributed to Fletcher, it is rash to suggest by a formula the qualities that are common to all of them. However, Fletcher's constant use of piquant themes and his skillful technique hit the taste of the élite Jacobean audience so well that many of his competitors, including Philip Massinger, Thomas Middleton, and John Ford, were impelled to change their practice and imitate him, and so to enlighten us as to his originality. We may say, then, that Fletcherian tragicomedies commonly offer a complicated intrigue in the setting of a remote court; the motives of passionate love, devoted friendship, and sacred honor clash, and the conflict produces agonies among the courtiers and sovereigns who are the chief persons. The king is often a tyrant; yet absolute submission to his adulterous or jealous will is the law of his society, and it is usually rendered. The fascination of incest, seduction, or sadism may be strongly introduced in the play, but the action normally moves to a happy ending by means of discoveries at the denouement both of unknown relationships and of disguised persons, as well as by abrupt changes of character from evil to good.

Some of these elements can be seen in a résumé of *Match Me in London*. In Seville, the lustful King of Spain falls in love with Tormiella, a shopkeeper's wife. After he has failed to win her by secret intrigue, he forces her to come to court as a lady-in-waiting to his virtuous queen.[32] No persuasion or threats can shake Tormiella's devotion to her husband, Cordolente, however, and she remains chaste (although the audience is misled for a while on this point).[33] By a ruse, the queen tricks the king into revealing his love for Tormiella and then angrily rebukes him, but in vain. He furthers his tyrannical passion by plotting to have the queen charged with adultery. He succeeds, then orders a physician to kill both the queen and Tormiella's husband.

[*80*]

But Doctor Lupo is a disguised revenger named Luke Gazetto. A rejected suitor of Tormiella, he has followed her and Cordo-lente to Seville from Cordoba, whence they had fled after their elopement and secret marriage. Lupo, who has been biding his time, weaves an involved intrigue at the climax of which Cor-dolente, deprived of his wife, will be duped into stabbing Tor-miella in the church while she is being married to the king. When this moment arrives, however, Cordolente recoils from desecrating the holy place with murder. Tormiella falls into his arms. A terrifying burst of thunder and lightning drives the royal party from the church before the marriage can take place. Following her talk with Cordolente, Tormiella is now able to in-form the king of Lupo's villainy. From the doctor the king learns that the queen still lives; he repents and gladly reunites Tor-miella and Cordolente.

Although the main plot is more complex than the preceding summary indicates, Dekker has added to it a political intrigue which is intended to stress the motif of personal honor clashing with loyalty to the sovereign. Valasco, the Admiral of Spain and the father of the wronged queen, has to repulse the treach-erous maneuvers of Prince John, the king's ambitious brother and an enemy of Valasco as well. Valasco frustrates the Prince by threats, challenges, and shrewd countermoves. This minor plot is so devoid of action and relies so much on conventions of mo-tive and situation that only careful reflection enables the modern reader to see its tensions. Nevertheless, both major and minor plots evidently dramatize the Fletcherian theme of a passion-ridden king who tyrannizes over subjects who may not resist his divinely given authority.

However, Dekker has modified many elements of his Jacobean play in an Elizabethan fashion. Tormiella, although of noble parentage, is a shopkeeper's wife and a faithful one; she resem-bles Jane, of *The Shoemaker's Holiday,* rather than the un-numbered lewd citizenesses of Jacobean comedy. Cordolente employs Bilbo, a voluble, comic servant of the same species as Shadow and Firke, though more subdued. Bilbo and a foolish courtier engage in a satirical debate on the vices of the court compared with those of the city. A number of scenes take place in Cordolente's shop, although it is true that they lack the realism introduced in *The Honest Whore*. After Tormiella has been carried off to the court, Cordolente, in disguise, identifies himself to his wife when he visits her to fit her with a pair of shoes—a device repeated from *The Shoemaker's Holiday*. Although the unhappy Queen of Spain is much more energetic than patient Grissil and Infelice, she is yet another example of the chaste, long-suffering wives whom Dekker admires. And, finally, the intricate plot, full of purposed seductions and murders, ends with only one death, that of one of the queen's servants. The king, Prince John, and Lupo repent; the queen, Valasco, Tormiella, and Cordolente forgive them. This conclusion in universal goodwill, appropriate for the romantic comedies of the 1590's, has not been well prepared for by humor of character or situation or by romantic sentiment. But, as we have said, the incongruity is usual in tragicomedy and is worth noting in *Match Me in London* only because the whole play lacks the geniality characteristic of Dekker.

Furthermore, *Match Me in London* lacks the strong moralism of Dekker's earlier plays as well as their implicit or expressed social criticism. It lacks also their patriotic feeling, warm sentiment, relish for absurdity of character, and passages of deep psychological realism. However, although this play may rightly be described as Dekker's attempt to please new tastes in drama which he did not really share, *Match Me,* like his earlier plays, displays his mastery of stagecraft. We may take for example an episode in Act II, Scene 4, which I have cited in a preceding paragraph—Tormiella's being taken to court. She enters the stage from Cordolente's house masked among a group of masked courtiers, men and women. She says only "Farewell!" to her husband who is standing aside with her father. Neither of them recognizes her. She goes off to court. When Cordolente and her father receive no response to their call for Tormiella, they enter the house and find her missing. The audience readily accepts this episode, including its brutal separation of young husband and wife, only because (1) it recognizes Tormiella when she detaches herself momentarily from the group for the farewell, though by convention her mask remains impenetrable for her husband and father; (2) the convention of drama is of absolute submission to the king's will, no matter how immoral; and (3) while the king, her would-be seducer, has already shown signs of remorse, Tormiella has shown signs of unyielding resistance to him. Her fidelity to Cordolente remains above question. Their separation, therefore, is not really tragic.

The frequent criticism that Dekker is weak in the construction of his plays may sometimes based on such scenes as the above from *Match Me in London* in which he relies quite successfully on the conventions of his theater, although partly to the mystification of the modern reader. In fact, with regard to his technique, Professor Harbage suggests that Dekker's practiced hand was the constructive one in several collaborated plays of high merit, such as *The Witch of Edmonton*.[34] The present chapter, it is hoped, may have produced evidence to support that view against the older, too offhand judgment that Dekker was either ignorant of dramatic art or disgracefully negligent of it—"shiftless and careless" in Swinburne's words—or "haphazard," unable to "devise perspectives of artifice," as Miss Bradbrook says.[35] Although no one will claim great merit for *Match Me in London*, an imitative play contrived by a weary veteran, it does show, like its predecessors, Dekker's mastery of dramatic technique.

We have completed our survey of the seven plays which scholars are almost unanimous in believing to be entirely Dekker's. They are the survivors of a large output, perhaps thirty-five or forty plays; for the fragmentary state of dramatic records permits only a guess as to how many Dekker wrote unaided. But we may probably assume, and validly, that these seven surviving plays are numerous and varied enough to represent Dekker's achievement fairly. Because the occupation of supplying the Elizabethan theaters often called for rapid composition, the playwrights commonly worked in teams. In the next chapter we shall examine four of Dekker's collaborated plays; we shall find that they support our conclusions about Dekker's artistic strength and weakness as these have been evaluated in his independent works.

CHAPTER 3

Dekker's Drama: Collaborations

I A Note on the Canon

WITH regard to the number of his collaborated and doubtfully ascribed plays, Dekker is not exceeded by many Elizabethan dramatists. The total number of works about which
question of his authorship arises—around fifteen—is more than
twice the number of those universally attributed to him—seven.
The canon of his surviving plays, therefore, is about twenty-two,
depending on the judgment of the scholar concerned. At least
ten other dramatists had a considerable share in the extant collaborated plays. However, because of present and, for our stated
aims, judicious limitations of space, a full explanation of the
kinds of evidence by which we detect Dekker's contributions will
not be undertaken. The student is referred to recent expositions
of the principles and techniques to be followed in solving problems of attribution, particularly by internal evidence,[1] and he is
reminded of the need for further studies in authenticity in the
Dekker canon. In the discussions in this chapter, as well as in
the ascriptions in the Bibliography (see Primary Sources), I shall
give my conclusions after brief citation of the evidence.

We shall also limit our criticism of Dekker's collaborations to
but four of the extant plays, the four most successful (along
with Part I of *The Honest Whore,* evaluated in Chapter 2). The
omission of about ten doubtful plays from this chapter, however,
will not seem so disturbing when we reflect that some of the ten
have been attributed to Dekker, probably erroneously, by only a
few scholars, and that most of the others, although truly belong-
ing in his canon, repeat less artistically themes and techniques
already described in Chapter 2. The four collaborations of acknowledged merit which we shall consider are *Patient Grissil;*

The Virgin Martyr; The Witch of Edmonton; and *The Sun's Darling.*

II *An Exemplum for the Public:* Patient Grissil *(1599)*

Patient Grissil was written for the Lord Admiral's Men, seemingly in December, 1599, by Henry Chettle, William Haughton, and Thomas Dekker.[2] The legend of the patient wife Griselda has been traced by scholars far back into the medieval period, and it appears in many later versions. It became the theme of the last story in Boccaccio's *Decameron,* of Chaucer's "The Clerk's Tale," of two Tudor plays, and of ballads and prose narratives in the Elizabethan age. Professor Harold Jenkins concludes that Dekker and his partners constructed their play out of general recollections of the legend but took certain details from a ballad published about 1593 in Thomas Deloney's *Garland of Goodwill.* A reader who compares the play with the versions in the *Decameron,* "The Clerk's Tale," and John Phillip's interlude of *Patient and Meek Griselda (circa* 1560) will agree that none of them seems to be followed very closely.

The story of Griselda resembles both a saint's legend and an allegory, and in the modern mind it gains more dignity if viewed in that light. The legend exalts the virtue of patience, not merely for the improvement of cranky wives, but for every Christian soul; it heartens the religious man by foretelling typologically the glorious reward that his immortal soul will enjoy once its earthly trials have been patiently endured and it is married forever to its divine spouse in Heaven. But here on earth there must first be undeserved suffering for the strengthening of virtue. In order to suggest the inscrutable ways of Providence in dealing with the soul, the legend rarely gives to Griselda's husband an adequate human motivation. In fact, both Chaucer and Boccaccio charge him with wanton cruelty, and today we may call it "sadism." But for the medieval and Renaissance audience, virtue triumphs over cruelty, and the ending is one of unalloyed happiness for all.

In *Patient Grissil,* Gwalther, Marquis of Salucia, has agreed to the request of his brother, the Marquis of Pavia, and other nobles that he choose a bride on a given day; and that day has now come. When they find him in the morning, garbed for hunting

as usual, they reproach him. But after Gwalther has extracted
from them a promise that they will not object to his choice, he,
in turn, promises to keep his word after the hunt. He does so by
leading the band to the cottage of old Janicola, the basket-
weaver. Gwalther has earlier observed the old man's beautiful
daughter, wooed her, found her virtuous, and has made his decision. He now comes to obtain Janicola's consent and to take
Grissil away.

However, the play has a minor theme, the testing and exposure
of false courtiers—in this instance, two flattering gentlemen
named Mario and Lepido who have also tried to woo the maid.
Gwalther tests all three, first asking Grissil to choose the hand-
somest man standing before her for her husband—himself, Mario,
or Lepido. She refuses on the score that she has no knowledge of
manly beauty. Doubtless her modesty and humility prevent her
from proclaiming her love of Gwalther. He then urges either of
the flatterers to take her for his wife as she stands in her home-
spun. (They themselves have been raised from poor estate.)
They refuse and thereby reveal not only the evil intent of their
wooing, but also their blindness to a pearl of true virtue in their
concern for wealth.

It remains for Gwalther to ask Janicola's consent to Grissil's
marriage. After one brief demur, Janicola submits to Gwalther's
vehement statement of his virtuous love. But Laureo, Janicola's
scholarly son, makes a stronger objection. Laureo has been nine
years at university, but has returned because of poverty to his
father's house, disheartened and bitter at the world's contempt
for learning. More fitly than anyone else he can state the prudent view of the marriage: "If equall thoughts durst both your
states conferre,/Her's is to lowe, and you to high for her" (I.2.262
–263). While Grissil does submit to her father's will, she remarks
ambiguously that she would rather remain her poor father's
daughter always. Gwalther understands a reference to her anxiety for the old man's future, and he promises to maintain her
father and brother in dignity. Before the whole party goes to the
palace for the wedding, Babulo, Janicola's clownish servant,
has his say; he expresses his fear that this wonder of the rich
loving the poor will last but nine days. Gwalther is not offended,
for he knows Babulo of old.

After one interlude of the farcical subplot (it also represents a lapse of months) comes Gwalther's abrupt decision to test his wife's meekness. He begins with minor humiliations to learn whether pride has corrupted her disposition since her marriage. He also tests Mario and Lepido again by pretending to hate Grissil and by asking their advice. They propose as a first step the banishment of Janicola and Laureo from court. Soon Grissil bears twins, a boy and a girl. While Grissil sleeps, Gwalther takes the infants from her; but, after much pleading with Furio, a servant in the Marquis's confidence, she is permitted to take the babes with her to Janicola's cottage. The hypocritical sorrow for Grissil expressed by Mario and Lepido is scorned by Gwalther. However, Furio and Gwalther, who is disguised, now come to the cottage and carry off the infants, supposedly to kill them, although actually they are to be reared by the Marquis of Pavia. Grissil's patience overcomes Laureo's and Babulo's desire to resist the cruelty.

Following another episode of *Patient Grissil's* underplot, Gwalther announces his intended marriage to the daughter of the Duke of Brandenberg and orders Grissil and her family to help prepare his house for the ceremonies; Grissil is even to crown the new bride. Laureo, however, rebels against having to fetch logs and is locked up; Janicola complains of his wrongs, but submits. At the climax Gwalther surprises his court by placing a crown on Grissil's head and a wreath on that of their daughter Gratiana, the supposed bride. The flattering courtiers are dismissed from court in disgrace, and Janicola and Laureo are restored to previous dignities.

Although in the preceding summary the subordinate plot is described as farcical, as it surely is, Professor Jenkins praises it not only for genuine humor, but as an appropriate emphasis on "wifely importance." It is, as he notes, another version of the taming of the shrew.[3] Sir Owen ap Meredith marries Gwenthyan, a Welsh widow, and assumes that henceforth he will rule the roost; but she destroys that idea with a series of violent rebellions that humiliate the blustery knight until he is on the point of knocking her brains out or running away from Gwalther's court (where all of this takes place). At the end, when Gwalther has crowned perfect meekness and patience in woman, he gives Sir Owen the wise counsel that an older woman cannot be schooled like a young one, she cannot be forced. Then Gwenthyan, to Sir Owen's surprise, announces that she has taught him his lesson and that he is the head; but she warns him not to "triumph too much and treade her . . . downe." If, then, patient Grissil is the type of precious meekness for all humanity, Gwenthyan bespeaks a complementary idea of justice: spouses are equal partners. The independence of women as persons is emphasized still more in a pleasant supplementary action (scarcely a plot) in which Julia, Gwalther's gay sister, after being wooed by three courtiers, decides to renounce the wars of marriage and lead apes in Hell.

Despite its very familiar story, *Patient Grissil* must have delighted its audience at the Fortune. The comedy successfully blends broad humor with elemental pathos, but, more importantly, it reaches the deepest idealism of its wide audience. Besides the reassurance that steadfast Christian virtue will receive its reward in this world as well as in the next, the fable charmed the spectators by a vital motif: the belief that a peasant maid may marry a prince—beauty and worth can break the bonds of custom. In an era when children of wealthy merchants were beginning to marry more frequently into the nobility, this motif had greater significance than at present.

Patient Grissil's purpose of spiritual edification, to teach everyone the love of patience, is accomplished and with some skill. As with most sermons, *Patient Grissil* pleases better because it gives voice to a virtue, namely, justice, that is rival to the thematic one; this is the function of the minor plot. The dramatists also wisely introduce two articulate characters not required by either plot—Laureo, the student, and Babulo, the clown. Although both are the source of humor, they also intersperse pungent commentary on the moralism of the patience-theme. Laureo, in particular, cannot be intended for any purpose other than to criticize a selfish noble class that pays too little reverence to learning and to question the unworldly submissiveness of saintly Grissil and Janicola. In this latter objection Laureo is wrong if his position is considered spiritually; but he speaks the audience's common sense just as Babulo sometimes speaks its vulgar skepticism, based on experience, about the rewards of vir-

tue. The high spiritual meaning of Grissil's life, therefore, is
shrewdly qualified by these mundane comments.

Characters who inject notes of reservation and humor into a
moral play are necessarily those who are most human. In this
class, besides Laureo and Babulo, are Sir Owen, Gwenthyan,
and Julia. It must be said, however, that none of the persons of
the play has as strong an individuality as we have found in
those of Dekker's unaided plays. The controlling theme of the
comedy, rather than the collaboration, probably causes this thin-
ness. Certainly the theme oversimplifies Grissil and Gwalther.
Even so, Grissil is not an automaton of virtue. When flattering
Mario praises Gwalther's wisdom, Grissil tartly comments to
Gwalther, "Your patience I commend that can abide,/To heare a
flatterer speake yet neuer chide" (II.2.146–147). Generally,
however, she is entirely submissive. Gwalther's cruelty, unex-
plained in terms of Elizabethan psychology, has been modified
by the device of his prolonged testing of the flattering courtiers,
and thereby an aspect of intelligence and virtue is given him.

Professor Jenkins praises *Patient Grissil* for "freshness and deli-
cacy not found in other Elizabethan versions" of the story, for the
sweetness of the verse, and for the "harmony and propriety of
tone which makes the whole comedy the work of art it is."[4] He
notes also the skill with which the subplots are interwoven and
the lively humor in them and in Babulo. Janicola's song, "Arte
thou poore yet hast thou golden Slumbers," has always been regarded as among the best of Elizabethan lyrics; another, a lullaby,
is but little inferior to it. The former has usually been assigned
to Dekker, but is ascribed to Chettle by Jenkins. On the whole,
Jenkins's praise of the play seems justified.

Curiously, the modern reader is apt to be displeased by two
things which Dekker and his partners would have thought to be
great merits: the prolonged testing of Grissil and the elaborate
use of Welsh dialect in the speech of Sir Owen and Gwenthyan.
Dekker would have said that the purpose of art is to teach a
moral lesson, and this comedy, while mingling the lesson with
delight, is a very clear teacher. Our objection stems possibly
from our unfamiliarity with the kind of moral discipline which
builds virtue by deliberately inflicting pain. As for the Welsh
dialect, unquestionably it is much more accurate and more

consistently used than in ninety-five per cent of Elizabethan drama; and its absurdities probably gave great entertainment at the Fortune. It has recently been attributed to Haughton.[5]

Although we can readily accept Professor Jenkins's remark that it is "very difficult to disentangle" the contributions of the three dramatists, his tentative assignment of their shares seems to be based on several mistaken inferences. As a single example, the fact that Chettle received the first payment for the play does not warrant the conclusion that he wrote the first scene. That Chettle acted as a sort of chairman may safely be inferred, but hardly more than that.[6] Professor Bowers reports that "there is common agreement that the main plot is Dekker's."[7] This is true, but not conclusive; in fact, the discrimination of the collaborators' shares is awaiting more careful study than it has yet received.

My own view, based on study of Dekker's spelling, versification, and diction, is that he wrote I.1, I.2, II.2, and III.1. On the basis of Professor Greene's study of Haughton's skillful use of dialect, Haughton wrote II.1, III.2, IV.3, and V.2. What is left is Chettle's: IV.1, IV.2, and V.1. Using the line numbering in the Bowers edition, we find that by these assignments Dekker contributed 757 lines, Haughton, 1,071, and Chettle, 570. Professor Bowers's opinion is that the manuscript sent to the printer was probably a transcription of the promptbook. It was apparently a fair copy, but probably not in the handwriting of any of the playwrights.

III Piety without Theology: The Virgin Martyr (1620)

After being licensed on October 6, 1620, and then produced at the Red Bull Theater by the Players of the Revels company, The Virgin Martyr was published in 1622 as written by Philip Massinger and Thomas Dekker. The literary qualities of the play fully support the title page ascription to these dramatists, and the textual peculiarities of the first edition clearly indicate a normal kind of collaboration, not a revision by Massinger of an old play by Dekker.[8] A theory of Massinger's revision can be based on evidence no more substantial than the fact that The Virgin Martyr utilizes a number of early Elizabethan dramatic traditions. In particular, it dramatizes a saint's legend and the psychomachia of the morality plays; furthermore, it presents on stage embodiments of two deadly sins, as well as an angel and the devil himself. Doubtless, however, these features should be attributed to Dekker's conception of the appropriate technique for exemplifying a religious theme to the audience at the Red Bull, a theater where older fashions in drama still prevailed.

We have noted in Chapter 1, moreover, that Dekker's religion was intensified by the suffering of his imprisonment and that this fervor was the source of the poem *Dekker's Dream* (1619). We may plausibly infer, then, that the idea of employing the legend of St. Dorothy originated in Dekker's devotional reading in prison or at home just after his release. But the method by which Dekker and Massinger composed the drama suggests that, before their partnership began, Dekker had done no more than outline the plot, scene by scene, if indeed, he had done that much; for all critics are agreed that Massinger wrote Act I. Therefore, it is undeniable that Massinger himself might have proposed the theme to Dekker.

The version of the legend which the dramatists used has not been identified. Jacobus de Voragine's *The Golden Legend* recounts Dorothea's martyrdom with much exaggeration and with differences of detail which indicate that, if Dekker and Massinger knew that book, they must have turned from it to a more primitive, simpler version of the legend. However, determining precisely which martyrology the collaborators drew upon is not indispensable for discerning the way in which they varied and added to the familiar pattern of this saint's life, which is paralleled in that of St. Winifred and others. We may begin by reviewing the plot of the play.

Sapritius, Roman governor of Caesarea in Cappadocia, has a brave son, Antoninus, whose service in Diocletian's army has won the emperor's favor for his father and himself. Above all, Antoninus's valor has attracted the love of Artemia, Diocletian's daughter, and she publicly chooses him for her husband. Her choice is a disaster for Antoninus, who loves Dorothea, a Christian virgin. Dorothea, however, rejects him. When Antoninus's friend, Macrinus, brings them together, she tells Antoninus that she loves another, far more wealthy and worthy than he; and she hopes to bring Antoninus to his service. This interview is doubly fatal, for it is secretly witnessed by Sapritius, Artemia, and the provost Theophilus, an old man chosen by Diocletian to discover and destroy the Christians in Caesarea. Harpax, servant and spy of Theophilus, has revealed Antoninus's love for Dorothea to Theophilus and Sapritius; but Harpax himself dares not come into her presence because of her heavenly young page, Angelo: "should I looke on him I must sinke downe."

Artemia is furious at being rejected for another woman, especially a Christian. However, acting with her absent father's authority, she commits Antoninus and Macrinus to Sapritius's custody and allows Theophilus to try to induce Dorothea to apostatize. The two daughters of Theophilus, Christeta and Caliste, formerly Christians, have apostatized, and so their father sends them to win Dorothea to paganism. But Dorothea, accompanied always by her friend Angelo, denounces the pagan gods and their religion as base idolatry. So eloquently does she speak that Christeta and Caliste, conscience-stricken, re-profess Christianity and a willingness for martyrdom. Meantime, Antoninus, a captive in his father's house, is plunged into love melancholy. Artemia, moved by pity, tells Sapritius that she forgives Antoninus and grants permission for him to marry Dorothea, should the maid renounce Christianity. Ironically, however, the ritual devotions to Jupiter at which Dorothea should publicly apostatize are climaxed when Christeta and Caliste throw down the god's image and spurn it. At Harpax's prompting, the enraged Theophilus kills his daughters in the presence of Artemia and Sapritius.

Sapritius then drags Dorothea by the hair into the chamber of his languishing son. He leaves her (and Angelo) there with the demand that Antoninus ravish her at once. But Antoninus abhors the sin. Sapritius, who has been watching from a hiding place, furiously commands a British slave to win his liberty by ravishing Dorothea; but the slave scorns such Roman baseness. While the maddened Sapritius beats Dorothea to the earth, he suddenly falls unconscious, one cheek blasted. Dorothea is dragged away to torture. Her chief tormentors are Hircius and Spungius, two villains whom she once saved from the gallows. Incited by Harpax, they attempt to beat her with cudgels, but Dorothea remains miraculously unhurt. Theophilus orders the wretches to be hanged, and Sapritius commands the execution of

Dorothea. The girl is brought to the scaffold in the presence of Antoninus and her enemies, including Harpax. In bitter hatred Theophilus asks her and Antoninus to send back some of its fruit to him after they have reached Paradise. Angelo appears to Dorothea and Harpax, though he is invisible to the rest; Harpax flees. Antoninus, miraculously restored to health, is able to kneel beside the block and to hold the martyr's hand as the axe falls. Then, as he had petitioned in prayer, he also dies.

A few days later, Theophilus, while gloating over the records of the cruelties used on Christian martyrs, especially in Britain, is surprised by the appearance of Angelo who is carrying a basket of fruit and flowers sent by Dorothea. Angelo vanishes. When Theophilus eats of the fruit, he is interrupted by Harpax who tries to reassert his power over him. But Theophilus has seized the graces offered him and forces the devil hellward by showing him a cross of heavenly flowers. Angelo greets Theophilus again with a promise of salvation. Later, Theophilus secretly releases all Christian captives from the prisons and sends them out to sea with Macrinus as their guide to freedom. Called by Diocletian to recount the circumstances of Dorothea's death, Theophilus proclaims her a martyr to true religion and himself a Christian. Thereupon he is racked in the presence of the emperor; and, when he dies, he is welcomed by Dorothea, Antoninus, his own daughters, and Angelo. Harpax, who witnesses this welcome, sinks to hell amid lightning flashes.

Evidently the heroic virtues, the endurance, and the miracles of Dorothea constitute one theme of the play; the conflict between divine grace and the devil's malice toward the souls of men —in particular, Theophilus's—constitutes the other. The two themes are, in effect, one: Dorothea's faith, hope, and charity are the means by which divine grace reaches and saves the souls of the other martyrs in spite of the spiritual knowledge and cunning of the devil Harpax. Because Dorothea, for dramatic purposes, is assured of salvation by the presence of Angelo, suspense is created chiefly by the destinies of those whom she influences. In them are exemplified the human relationships and weaknesses from which Dorothea has been freed. She has no family whose fate is involved with hers, and her love is given only to a heavenly lover.

[*93*]

In contrast, Antoninus's carnal passion for Dorothea must be transmuted into a wholly spiritual love. His father's misunderstanding and resentment of him are paralleled and developed in Theophilus's relations with his daughters. In this way Dorothea's peculiar isolation from human connections is suppressed, as it were. Instead, the psychological problems of the Christian martyr are revealed in their major aspects in the struggles of her disciples, while the source of the sufferings—divine grace embodied in Dorothea and Angelo—is given full dramatic impact by symbolic characters. If family relationships had complicated Dorothea's martyrdom with tragic psychological stresses, we would have a play less elemental and emphatic in its religious statement. Since spiritual edification was certainly the primary purpose of Dekker and Massinger, we cannot object to the structure they have borrowed from the morality tradition.

We should come to the same conclusion about the element of comedy in *The Virgin Martyr*, which is much reduced from its usual prominence in early Elizabethan interludes. The comic element is generated by only two characters, Hircius (whose name is equivalent to "lechery") and Spungius ("drunkenness"), the deadly sins of lust and gluttony; but it is manifested more in talk than in action. In fact, their exchanges are self-descriptions of the kind spoken by these qualities in morality plays; briefer specimens are uttered by the Seven Deadly Sins in Marlowe's *Doctor Faustus*. Dekker (generally thought to be the author of these scenes) has greatly elaborated and given a pseudo-dramatic semblance to the descriptions. The humor is obscene, and Dekker has made it disgusting in order to highlight the two gallows-birds as hateful embodiments of sin and as repulsive counterparts to sanctity and grace. But their by-play in the interviews with Angelo and their ineffective attempt to cudgel Dorothea have a crude, ironic humor.[9] Because of their malice, the two villains might seem to be offspring of both the Deadly Sins and the Vice of the moralities; but they are not intriguers and are too stupid to represent the Vice.

To describe the play as a belated piece of medieval didacticism would be to ignore its relation to its own era, as well as more important questions: What are its merits as a work of art which aims to disclose both the suffering and the significance of martyrdom? Does the play have the impact hoped for by the dramatists? We shall shortly consider its popularity as an indication of its contemporary impact. As to its power for later generations, we may recall that our century has produced a number of great plays on martyrdom, several of them in English. By way of comparison, in purpose and technique *The Virgin Martyr* lies between T. S. Eliot's *Murder in the Cathedral* and Robert Bolt's *A Man for All Seasons*. *The Virgin Martyr* does not disclose the inward struggle of the martyr's spirit against his unruly will as does Eliot's play, but it does resemble *Murder in the Cathedral* in offering a symbolic statement of the martyr's conflict. *The Virgin Martyr* resembles *A Man for All Seasons* in exemplifying the human attachments in the martyr's feelings; but by generalizing this aspect and by emphasizing the inevitable triumph of grace, it loses the tragic interest of Thomas More's sufferings in his historical dilemma. Although we may feel a much greater intensity in both of these modern dramas, we must allow for the archaic technique that operates against our full response to *The Virgin Martyr*.

Inevitably, we must also evaluate *The Virgin Martyr* in terms of religious assumptions. We find it sincere but shallow in its conceptions, and therefore not very moving. The great mysteries of the Christian religion are not impressed on us by the play—the human nature and death of the Savior and his legacy of corporate worship and sacraments are not mentioned; in fact, the name of Jesus does not occur. The difficulty is deeper than simply the use of paraphrases to conform to the law forbidding the use of divine names on the stage; the trouble is that the religiosity of the play has been detached from the specific doctrines and symbols of Christian faith which arouse imagination and feeling. There is no love-feast of the faithful, no comforting of captives in prison, no visit from a missionary, no secret bringing of sacraments.

In short, there is no Church; the saints in *The Virgin Martyr* are not members of a communion on earth and in heaven; the religion has been somewhat denatured. Marlowe, in contrast, while writing in the same era of controversy, did not fear to concentrate on the theological mystery of the operation of grace in the soul of Doctor Faustus. Dekker and Massinger's

portrayal of the anguish of martyrdom is blurred with generalized pious feeling. True, *The Virgin Martyr* has unity of theme
and action, but the playwrights have lost touch with or put aside
theology. In this respect, the play seems, to its detriment,
naïve.

In adapting their style to the theme, the two dramatists are
comparable, for neither achieves a remarkable success. Massinger's masculine blank verse does well for scenes of mundane
drama and familiar emotion; and, of course, the prosodic energy
remains when he is aiming at more sublime ideas. But he never
really rises above vigorous rhetoric, sound but commonplace
thought, and familiar allusion. Of Dorothea's death Theophilus
(now the martyr) says:

> [She] lost no husband in whose ouerthrow
> Her wealth and honour suncke, no feare of want
> Did make her being tedious, but aiming
> At an immortal crowne, and in his cause
> Who onely can bestow it; who sent downe
> Legions of ministring Angels to beare vp
> Her spotlesse soule to heauen; who entertaind it
> With choyce celestiall musicke, equall to
> The motion of the spheres.... (V.2.126–134)

Although Dekker commonly has more capacity for tenderness
than Massinger, he is no more gifted with language of tragic intensity. Dekker wrote the scene in which Theophilus, visited
by Angelo, repents his crimes of cruelty. The episode is an exact counterpart to that of unrepentant Faustus in his last agony,
even to the presence of the threatening devil-master. In contrast to Faustus, however, Theophilus achieves hope in God's
mercy:

> At thee ile fling that *Iupiter,* for me thinkes
> I serue a better Master, he now checkes me
> For murthering my two daughters, put on by thee;
> By thy damn'd Rhetoricke did I hunt the life
> Of *Dorotea,* the holy Virgin Martyr,
> She is not angry with the Axe nor me,
> But sends these presents to me, and ile trauell
> Ore worlds to finde her, and from her white hand
> To beg a forgiueness. (V.1.142–150)

The comparison with *Doctor Faustus* is very probably one that Dekker consciously but unfortunately intended. In conclusion, we must say that the poetry of *The Virgin Martyr* falls below the skill of its dramaturgy.

The dramatists' shares in the composition of *The Virgin Martyr* have been assigned by its editors with remarkable unanimity. This is explained both by the idiosyncrasy of Massinger's blank verse and by the fact that he has left us a play wholly in his own handwriting—*Believe As You List*—from which reliable knowledge of Massinger's spelling, punctuation, and other graphic habits can be derived. Robert Boyle, William Gifford, and Fredson Bowers have ascribed to Massinger Act I, Act III, Scenes 1 and 2, and Act V, Scene 2. Rather certainly, then, Massinger wrote the opening of the play, the conversion and martyrdom of Theophilus's daughters, and the martyrdom of Dorothea. Dekker seems to have written all of Act II, Act III, Scene 3, Act IV, Scene 2, and Act V, Scene 1. These scenes originate and develop the characters of Harpax, Hircius, and Spungius; but Dekker also presented the heroism of Dorothea under torture (IV.2) and the conversion of Theophilus (V.1).

Act IV, Scenes 1 and 3, have remained the only really doubtful portions. Professor Bowers tentatively ascribes IV.1 to Dekker, perhaps as reviser of Massinger's original draft; Massinger, however, seems to be the author of the substance of IV.3. If we assign Scene 1 to Dekker and Scene 3 to Massinger, the dramatists' shares in *The Virgin Martyr* total, for Massinger, 1,257 lines, and for Dekker, 1,305 lines. The difference is only 48 lines. Even if both doubtful scenes are assigned to one or the other dramatist, the difference totals only about 238 lines. More interesting than this equality of contribution, however, is the additional evidence that in some collaborations Elizabethan playwrights divided the work not by plots, but by themes and episodes, a procedure possible only after fairly careful planning.

Dramatic records indicate that *The Virgin Martyr* was popular. The title page of the first edition says that the play was acted "divers times"; and in 1624 an additional scene (not in the extant version) was licensed for a revival. Before the revival, however, the play was published in 1622. More surprisingly, it was republished in 1631, 1651, and 1661, and it was finally adapted for eighteenth-century taste under the title of *Injured Virtue, or the Virgin Martyr* by Benjamin Griffin in 1715. Evidently the religiosity of this play satisfied the piety of a large segment of the English public during the century of the Puritan conflict. *The Virgin Martyr* is as truly a document in the history of English culture as is *The Whore of Babylon.*

IV *Domestic Tragedy:* The Witch of Edmonton *(1621)*

About a year after contributing to *The Virgin Martyr,* Dekker joined William Rowley and John Ford in composing *The Witch of Edmonton.*[10] Like other collaborations involving three or more playwrights, *The Witch* was probably written rapidly to take advantage of current excitement about the trial of Elizabeth Sawyer of Edmonton, a town lying a few miles north of London. A tract that described the "discovery" of the witch, published in the spring of 1621, was used by the dramatists. The production of the play at court on December 29, 1621, is not likely to have been the first one; the Prince's Men, for whom *The Witch of Edmonton* was written, had no doubt presented it several times already at the Cock-pit, a private theater which they were occupying in 1621.

Although *The Witch of Edmonton* has stronger dramatic merits, it is a less unified work than *The Virgin Martyr;* in fact, it has two quite distinct plots. In the major one, a domestic tragedy, young Frank Thorney has taken service in the household of Sir Arthur Clarington and has fallen in love with a waiting-maid, Winnifride. At the beginning of the play Winnifride has just revealed her pregnancy to Frank, and the couple has secretly been married. But the marriage may not be publicized until Frank has won his father's consent to a union that will bring little financial gain. Winnifride has also been Sir Arthur's paramour, and Sir Arthur proposes to continue the affair unknown to Frank. Touched, however, by Frank's sincerity, Winnifride has a change of heart and firmly repulses Sir Arthur. She goes to live with an uncle until Frank can win his father's approval.

Meantime, Old Thorney has negotiated an advantageous marriage for Frank with Susan Carter, daughter of a well-to-do yeoman of Hertfordshire, near Edmonton. Susan Carter's dowery, as Old Thorney tells Frank, is absolutely necessary to save the father from ruin; the Thorney lands are mortgaged disastrously. Furthermore, Susan has already fallen in love with Frank. She is quick to reject Master Warbeck who has come a-wooing along with Somerton, the lover of Susan's sister, Katherine. And Old Carter dislikes Warbeck, but likes Frank. Under all this pressure, Frank agrees to a marriage he knows is bigamous.

Once the marriage ceremony has been performed and the financial settlement made, Frank plans secretly to flee at once with Winnifride to "some other Nation." He tells Susan of a journey he simply must make without her. Dressed as a page, Winnifride joins Frank at his home and receives Susan's injunctions to watch over her husband. Winnifride rides on ahead, leading Frank's horse. Susan is so loth to part from Frank that she accompanies him too far, to a dangerously lonely spot. Old Thorney and Old Carter are following some distance behind to fetch Susan home again. To free himself from the false marriage, to avoid the necessity of lifelong exile, and to gain the full enjoyment of her property, Frank conceives the idea of killing Susan. He confesses his deceptions and his purpose to her; she prepares for death; and he stabs her.

Frank then wounds himself and binds himself to a tree. When the two fathers arrive on the scene, Frank accuses Warbeck and Somerton of murdering Susan and of attempting to kill him. Warbeck and Somerton are jailed to await trial. Meanwhile, at Old Carter's house Frank, confined to bed because of his wounds, is ill with melancholy brought on by remorse. Susan's sister, Katherine, who is nursing him, after setting food before him, looks in his pocket for his knife and finds one that is bloodstained. While she is gone to accuse Frank to her father, Winnifride comes, still disguised as a page, and Frank confesses the murder to her. Old Carter brings Susan's body to Frank and accuses him. Frank denies it, however, until Winnifride tells Carter that her husband has confessed it to her. Frank is imprisoned, tried, and condemned. On the way to the gallows he meets and asks pardon of his father, Winnifride, Old Carter, Warbeck, and Somerton. Old Carter forgives Winnifride and takes her into his home.

[*99*]

Frank's tragedy is not one that requires the tangible presence of supernatural beings. But in the other plot the witch of Edmonton's sorcery demands, of course, the appearance of the devil as a dramatic person, here in the shape of a black dog. Old Elizabeth Sawyer, "poor, deform'd and ignorant," is the victim of slanders, ostracism, hatred, and blows from the folk who live around Edmonton. Their cruelties make her wish to be what they think she is; and the black dog gifted with speech, comes to her. They make a covenant, he promising to be her revenger, she giving her soul to him, in sign of which he sucks blood from her arm. However, Elizabeth finds the devil less potent than she had expected: he can blight crops and sicken cattle, but he cannot touch men directly unless they consent to his presence.

The witch is unable, therefore, to strike her worst enemy, Old Banks. When Bank's foolish son, Cuddy, comes to her for help in his wooing of Katherine Carter, a demon, in the form of Katherine, leads him into a pond in the dark. Nevertheless, Cuddy strikes up a friendship with the black dog and invites him to take part the next day in a morris dance, at Sir Arthur Clarington's house. There the morris men dance, symbolically, to the fiddling of the devil, and Sir Arthur is a witness of the merriment. Meantime, the boors continue their persecution of Mother Sawyer. In retaliation, she commands the dog to cast a spell on a neighbor, Anne Ratcliffe. As a result, Mrs. Ratcliffe runs mad, escapes her friends' control, and beats out her brains. Sir Arthur has joined the ranks of the witch's enemies. Old Banks obtains a warrant for her arrest; the black dog abandons her as already his prey; she is tried, condemned, and goes to her death execrated by all, even by Old Carter. Alternately she craves vengeance on her enemies and asserts her repentance for her sorcery.

The two plots are linked somewhat less well than usual by the presence of characters active in both. In fact, this medium is practically limited to two scenes: Sir Arthur's very minor intervention in the witch's arraignment; and the symbolic coming of the black dog to Frank Thorney's side. Yet the dramatists seemingly intended a thematic parallelism between the two actions, as is further evidenced by a couplet, "The whole Argument," which someone (possibly none of the dramatists) prefixed to the first edition: "Forc'd Marriage, Murder; Murder, Blood requires: Reproach, Revenge; Revenge, Hells help desires."

To establish these parallels, we have Frank Thorney's decision criminally to deceive Susan, her father, and his own father in order to obtain the money he needs for flight with Winnifride; thus he robs Susan of dowery, honor, and happiness. In the following scene Mother Sawyer decides to give reign to her hatred and to yield her body to the devil in order to revenge herself on the rustics. After Frank's wedding to Susan, the pair has a conversation that is a little comedy of ironic errors: Susan detects Frank's anxiety and remorse as he thinks of his coming flight, but she attributes his disturbance to some defect in herself and asks time for reform. Frank mistakenly calls her "Winnifride" instead of "Susan" and blunderingly announces a necessary but mysterious journey for the day after the wedding. Susan concludes that Warbeck has challenged him to a duel.

Corresponding in tone, the following scene has Cuddy Banks foolishly pursuing his demonic phantom lover and tumbling into a pond. Again, in Act IV, Scene 2, Frank's fate is determined by Katherine's providential discovery of the knife and his confession to Winnifride; in the following scene, V.1, the witch discovers the deceit of the devil, who leaves her helpless, and she is carried off to jail by the rustics. Finally, Frank's procession to the scaffold is broken into two parts separated by a scene in which Mother Sawyer is on her way to execution.

These deliberate similarities of action and tone would doubtless have more effect in the theater than in the reading. Yet they are not strong and precise enough to be deemed good craftsmanship. And they are further weakened by William Rowley's proneness to expand comic dialogue, particularly that in which he was to have a part (it has very plausibly been suggested that he acted Cuddy). His prolonged drolling perhaps contributed greatly to the audience's pleasure, but we may still believe that it dulls esthetic effects and diminishes tragic feeling. Structurally, then, *The Witch of Edmonton* is not highly impressive.

Of course, there is no novelty in our conclusion that the mastery in this drama appears most in the psychological truth of motivation and emotion in the characters, although that fact is surprising, considering the origin of the play. The most striking of the characters are Susan, Frank, and Mother Sawyer, but the portraits of Winnifride, Old Carter, and Katherine are also excellent. It is not surprising that four of these are women, for both Dekker and Ford generally show unusually sympathetic understanding of women in their other plays. In Susan the combined traits of devotion, humor, tenderness, candor, humility, purity of heart, independence of mind, and courage make an irresistible personality which almost brings Frank to confession on the very eve of his flight with Winnifride. Susan is the equal of Perdita in *The Winter's Tale,* except for Perdita's gift of lyric poetry.

Although Frank's brutal murder of Susan might be expected to leave us convinced that he is a moral monster, this is not the case. Unlike the character and motives of Giovanni in Ford's *'Tis Pity She's a Whore,* Frank's character and motives are kept on a very familiar and plausible level. True, we are aware of corruption in his soul before his consent to marry Susan; he shows it by asking Sir Arthur Clarington to write a lying letter to Frank's father, denying the marriage to Winnifride. The request dishonors Sir Arthur (though he accedes to it); the letter may dishonor Winnifride. The fact that Frank has been Sir Arthur's dupe does not excuse this baseness. On the other hand, we have already noted the manifold pressures that make credible his entrance into the bigamous marriage, which, of course, he has never intended. His reproachful conscience leads him deliberately to hurt Susan at the same time that he is planning the abandonment that will ruin her life. His ingrained respect for virtue and sanctity forces him to warn Susan that he is about to kill her, both that she may prepare for death and that she may not think he has *premeditated* the crime—a remarkable touch (III.3.22–33). Furthermore, Frank's sense of guilt drives him to confess the murder to Winnifride, although a desperate hope of saving life and pleasure makes him deny his crime when Winnifride betrays the confession to Old Carter. This strong activity of conscience in a young man governed by egoism, passion, and unscrupulousness, like the similar paradox in Macbeth, makes powerful drama; it also makes credible Frank's final repentance.

The character of Elizabeth Sawyer depends to some extent on

notions of witchcraft implicit in the play, and these should be commented on briefly. The sixteenth-century controversy over the reality of witchcraft, which is reflected in a number of earlier plays, including *Macbeth,* gained further interest in England because of King James's concern with the subject in his book, *Daemonologie* (1597). Dekker, Ford, and Rowley, who were practical playwrights like Shakespeare, assumed that most of their audience believed witchcraft was not only theoretically possible but even that it occurred from time to time. The question of whether it had occurred in many or few of the cases reported was irrelevant; dramatically, the problem was how to deal with the case of Elizabeth Sawyer. The dramatists' decision was to show her as an actual witch; therefore the devil, as a person, must deal with Mother Sawyer and make a contract with her. To depict the hag as simply the pitiable victim of rustic stupidity and cruelty would not have corresponded thematically to Frank's deliberate evildoing and would have lost the tragic force of an equally deliberate choice of crime by Mother Sawyer. We may note that actual witchcraft also adds suspense, for the devil's effort to secure the sorcerer's damnation is a struggle against God's grace and the witch's free will—a combat that could go either way.

Although everyone is struck with the play's eloquent protest against the cruelty practiced on lonely old women in country places, the protest clearly does not deny that such beldames may be witches; it asserts that cruelty makes them adopt witchcraft:

> Some call me Witch;
> And being ignorant of my self, they go
> About to teach me how to be one: urging,
> That my bad tongue (by their bad usage made so)
> Forespeaks their Cattle, doth bewitch their Corn,
> Themselves, their Servants, and their Babes at nurse.
> This they enforce upon me: and in part
> Make me to credit it. (II.1.8–15)

Our modern pity for abandoned old women branded as witches in the sixteenth and seventeenth centuries was obviously also felt by sensitive people in those times—including a recognition

[*103*]

of the beldames' self-delusion. However, Englishmen of 1620 did not dismiss the old women's moral responsibility for attempted or achieved complicity with the devil or, for that matter, their guilt for idle threats or scurrility of tongue (IV.1.70–81). The boors' sins of cruelty do not excuse the beldames' malice. This insistence on responsibility is but another evidence of the moral clarity from which Elizabethan drama in general derives much of its stamina.

Like most protagonists of that drama, Mother Sawyer speaks in blank verse with an eloquence that in reality, of course, she would not possess; in fact, she may be said to be almost depersonalized in the expressiveness with which she describes the cruelties which have isolated her and fill her with resentment (II.1.1–13, 94–115). According to most critics, it is Dekker who provides her even with diatribes against lechers in court and city, shrews, dishonest lawyers, seducers—all included under "that universal Name" of witch (IV.1.101–144). But, as an expression of her sufferings and anger, this eloquence has great power because it utters our own painful dramatic experience of the rustics' brutal treatment and of corrupt Sir Arthur's secret malice against her and her truth-speaking. In this suffering the witch shows sensitivity, courage, and a pathetic desire for friendship even with her familiar demon. Her character is a simple one, yet vivid, not deadened by senility or privation.

Whichever dramatist wrote the episode of Mother Sawyer's going forth to execution succeeded in brilliantly maintaining her qualities. Even in her last hour of life the rustics follow along, berating her, and the cry is taken up by Old Carter, who accuses her of witching the devil into Frank. She shrieks: "... Cannot a poor old woman/Have your leave to die without vexation?/ ... Have I scarce breath enough to say my Prayers?/ And would you force me to spend that in bawling?" (V.3.24–25, 48–49). Her repentance, attained with such difficulty, is soon upset by revived anger against the injustice and vindictiveness of her persecutors. Although she lies when she denies bewitching Anne Ratcliffe (IV.1.168–176, V.3.33), still Mother Sawyer did not directly cause Anne's death; so that her lie results from fear or confusion, not malice. We are meant to believe that, like Frank, Mother Sawyer will be saved. The black dog has disappeared, and the old woman's last words are: "Bear witness, I repent all former evil;/There is no damned Conjurer like the Devil" (V.3.50–51).

In early seventeenth-century England almost no one questioned the reality of the devil as a person; and in every witch play the devil had to appear. But in what shape? Whether he comes as Mephostophilus, Pug, Friar Rush, or black dog, the play at once veers toward comedy because no theatrical shape can express the horror of the devil in the believer's imagination. The gap between mental image and stage semblance creates humor. Mephostophilus is ironic, the black dog merely grotesque; but both are inadequate, and their difference is just a matter of degree. For this reason, probably, the collaborators saw little advantage in sophisticating the personage of Mother Sawyer's tempter; they followed their source, Henry Goodcole's *Wonderful Discovery of Elizabeth Sawyer,* with but minor changes in the use of the dog. Rowley, then, could turn the comic guise to advantage by having Cuddy Banks conceal his fear and pretend that Satan is only a friendly beast as he advises him to mend his ways. The employment of the dog, even though symbolically, in the tragic plot was a mistake, however, because it seriously violates the tone.

No scholar of authority has so far felt very confident of being able to distinguish the contributions of the three collaborators on *The Witch.* Few students are likely to question the usual assumption that Rowley composed most of the episodes in which Cuddy Banks figures, especially that with the morris dancers, III.4; but not all scenes in which Cuddy appears need be Rowley's contribution. However, general agreement holds for his authorship of III.1 and III.4; he may also have contributed to II.1, III.3, and IV.1.[11] Fairly strong agreement assigns I.1 to Ford, and I.2 is also given to him or, in some way, jointly to him and Dekker. Dekker is probably the author of IV.1, although Rowley may have written the episode with Cuddy at the end.

Other than these tentative ascriptions, the major part of the play remains in doubt. But the doubt need not last forever. If Professor Bowers's hypothesis is correct that the printer set type from the dramatists' autographs or a close transcription of them,[12] enough morphological clues to each contributor's handwriting (as well as stylistic traits) must remain for brains and computers to settle finally the problem of ascription. A partial offset to this textual authenticity in the quarto is the fact that it was printed so late in the seventeenth century, 1658, that the compositors felt freer to modernize the archaic forms they encountered in these manuscripts written by playwrights long dead.

V A Dramatic Apologue: The Sun's Darling (1624)

About 1624 Dekker and Ford collaborated on a number of plays; records of four of them establish the fact of partnership, but only one of the four survives: *The Sun's Darling: A Moral Masque*.[13] This is perhaps the best of the small group of plays called "theater masques," in which a mythic story is the vehicle for frequent singing and dancing as well as for lavish, symbolic costumes, but for which no spectacular stage décor was provided. The absence of elaborate settings and of full choruses and orchestras constituted the major difference in production between the theater masque and the court masque. In the theater, story and eloquent expression inevitably became more important than in the court masque. The didactic purpose, which in earlier generations had created the morality play, expressed itself in more humanistic style in the theater masque.[14]

The fable in *The Sun's Darling* opens with young Raybright, child of the Sun, asleep and indulging his faculty of fancy in dreams. Awakened by a priest of the Sun, Raybright proclaims his cynical disillusionment with the accepted values of the world; but the priest tells him: " 'Tis melancholy, and too fond indulgence/To your own dull'd affections, sway your judgment. . . ." (I.1.62–63). The priest promises that the Sun himself is coming to offer all good gifts to his child. Before the Sun arrives, Father Time appears, scourging Folly in the person of a wastrel gallant and trying to drive the prodigal from the world. But Folly is impudent and persistent, and because he is a distant cousin of the Moon, he claims an important place in the world, and in many guises. Time gives up the attempt, the Sun comes to offer all his gifts, and Raybright asks if he may, "for one onely year,/Enjoy the several pleasures here,/Which every season in his kinde,/Can bless a mortal with" (I.1.188–191). Because this request has been bred of reason, the Sun gladly grants it. The priest leads Raybright to the garden of Spring, and Folly, uninvited, follows after.

Now begins Raybright's experience of the gifts of the four seasons, gifts which may be enjoyed rationally and healthfully —or be corrupted by unreason. Spring comes, accompanied by Youth, Health, and Delight, to welcome Raybright with the rustic music of cornets, a cuckoo song, and a morris dance. Spring's daughter May is to be the young man's companion; but while Spring has gone to fetch her, Folly tells Raybright that an empress, Lady Humor, has fallen in love with the Sun's darling. Lady Humor presently comes with her train: a soldier, a Spanish confectioner, an Italian dancer, and a French tailor. When Spring returns, Raybright, completely under the spell of Humor (irrational caprice), jeers at that "goodie herb-wife" and goes off with Humor and Folly.

Ironically, he now becomes capricious. Although he regrets the loss of Spring and finds Humor a common thing, a whore, it is not hard for Humor and Folly to resubjugate him. They next arrive in the domain of Summer, the Sun's queen. Informed of Raybright's behavior, Summer is indignant at his treatment of her nurse, the Spring. When the Sun urges her to indulge his child, Summer offers Raybright more rustic song and dance and all her gifts, even though at first she cannot forgive the double-dealer. Then Summer relents and appeals for Raybright's love. When he rejects her, too, the Sun commands Cupid and Fortune to take charge of wanton Raybright. As they lead him to Autumn, Humor and Folly trail after him.

Pomona, queen in Autumn's kingdom, feasts Raybright to his stomach's content; and Autumn himself welcomes the youth with wassail and dances. Cupid and Fortune promise him untold gifts; but Humor and Folly, not to be eluded, reappear and persuade befuddled Raybright to leave Autumn and to dwell in the North with more splendid Winter. At this point (Act V, Scene 1), someone has inserted a scene of political allusion: the peasants from the North threaten Raybright if he comes to their land (as Scotsmen resented Charles I's coming, in the Bishops' War, 1638–1640).

Winter rebukes these boors, and his queen, Bounty, offers

Raybright lavish entertainment that begins with a simplified masque of The Four Elements and the Four Humors shown reconciled to one another and at peace. But Lady Humor is jealous and, as a last resort, suggests to Raybright that he abandon Winter, go back to Spring, and retrace the course of the year, imitating his father. Raybright happily assents. With that, the Sun comes to deny the repetition and to sum up the meaning of the fable. Nature has provided man with Youth, Health, Delight, and all desirable things; Humor and Folly are the enemies of peace and happiness.

Morally and philosophically, Raybright represents man responding to the beneficence of Nature as she revolves through the four seasons. To accept the gifts of the present season is the way to health and peace—*O sweet content!* as Dekker sang in *Patient Grissil*. But to repine for the benefits of other times is irrational and unhealthful. More broadly, the play depicts man in his general relations with Nature; she provides plenteously for him, and his pursuit of luxuries and frivolities is irrational. The epistle to the reader of this play warns that *"It is not here intended to present thee with the perfect Analogy betwixt the World and man, which [the world] was made for Man...."* Nevertheless, our contented acceptance of the substantial, if simple, benefits that Nature is ready to provide seems to be the commonplace moral that is on the surface of this fable.

The epistle goes on to trace man through the four seasons— "the Twy-light of his age," "the Noone-tide," "his Autumne," and "the Winter, or his nonage"—and, at the last, *"Folly and Humour,* Faine hee'd cast away,/But they will never leave him, till hee's *Clay"* (lines 24-25). As a picture of the four ages of man, the play informs us that in the winter of his life man has wisdom enough to live life well and to bring the microcosm of elements and humors within him into harmony with itself and with outer Nature—if only he could repeat the cycle of his seasons! Momentarily suppressing this note of irony, Ford (probably it was he) wrote a beautiful final couplet: "Man hath a double guard, if time can win him;/Heavens power above him, his own peace within him." The clause, "if time can win him," presumably is to be completed with "ever to see the truth"; but irony remains the dominant note of the last scene. Man,

[108]

grown wise too late, unable to shake off lifelong folly, denied just one more chance—this is the theme. Even the argument between Conceit (poetic imagination) and Detraction about the merits of the Masque of the Elements and Humors makes an oblique comment on the pretensions of Ford and Dekker to philosophy in *The Sun's Darling*: "What goodly thing is't, in the name of laughter?" asks Detraction (V.I.206–207).

The same genial irony amuses us in the preceding acts. In II.1, when Spring offers Raybright the lyric delights of birdsong—the lark "shall be thy tenant, call thee Lord,/And for her rent pay thee in change of songs"—he jeeringly replies, "I must turn bird-catcher." Spring promises him poetic inspiration; but again he scoffs, "Live by singing ballets?" (229–231, 248). Similarly, the description of the luscious diet of fruits provided by Autumn is punctuated by Folly's ribald comments on the flatulence it is causing him. Of course, such discords are introduced by the dramatists for the delight of the contrast, not in real derogation of their central theme. On the contrary, the truth is that by the discordances the dramatists clarify the moral idea. As the satiric comments originate either directly with Folly and Humor or indirectly with them through their power over Raybright, these notes serve the same purpose as the antimasque in a court masque: to illuminate the ideal by contrast with the irrational.

In one aspect *The Sun's Darling* presents us the traditional Prodigal Son theme once again, but with a more humanistic and a wittier rendering. Ignoring all religious implications, the ironic myth instructs us about man's nature and relation to the physical world as understood by conventional learning. Yet the apologue is suggestive rather than strictly logical or philosophical; for instance, the analogy of the four ages of man with the seasons is very loose (as the epistle, quoted in a preceding paragraph, implies). However, the parallel to the Prodigal Son dallying with his harlot (Lady Humor behaves like a jealous stage-courtesan) and with the wastrel gallant, Folly, recalls for the audience not only the comedy of that medieval tradition but its deep moral significance. The parable of Raybright's errors is therefore enriched. It is also adorned by poetic eloquence. Humor thus describes the land of Summer:

> [You will find there] All the quiristers
> That learn't to sing i'th Temple of the *Spring;*
> But there attain such cunning, that when the windes
> Rore and are mad, and clouds in antick gambols
> Dance o're our head, their voices have such charms,
> They'l all stand still to listen. (III.2.21–26)

This passage fairly represents the level of the verse. The play also has several delightful songs. All in all, a reader who turns from one of the best of Jonson's court masques to *The Sun's Darling* will not be disappointed by a marked inferiority of style or substance in Dekker and Ford's play.

The hypothesis in vogue a generation or more ago that under the title *The Sun's Darling* Ford revised an early play of Dekker's called *Phaeton* has been generally rejected by recent critics as untenable, considering the evidence for the recent cooperation of Ford and Dekker in the early 1620's. If we assume, instead, that *The Sun's Darling* is a collaboration in the usual sense, it appears to me that Ford's contributions were probably Acts I and IV in their entirety and Act V from line 141 to 342, the end. (Each of the acts has but one scene.) As it stands, the opening episode of Act V is an interpolation or a revision made in 1638 or 1639 to satirize the Scots; possibly the rewritten passage ends at line 190, where all allusion to Scotland disappears, rather than at 140. Lines 1–140 do not seem to preserve distinguishable vestiges of the style of either dramatist; but the fifty lines, 140–190, may be a revision of Dekker's original.

To Dekker should be assigned Acts II and III. I think it plausible to believe that he dramatized Raybright's reception in Winter's domain, corresponding to the present lines 1–190 of Act V, and left the masque-within-the-play and the dénouement to Ford. Conjecturally, then, Dekker composed about 809 lines altogether, Ford about 663. The total of lines in the play as we have it is 1,472.

The Sun's Darling appears to be Dekker's last surviving play, but certainly not the last that he wrote either independently or jointly during the remaining decade of his life. The titles and dates of the lost plays are listed under "Primary Sources" in the Bibliography. Beyond the facts there stated, we know so little about those works that conjecture about them is unprofitable.

With regard to his entire career, reliable records give the names of at least fourteen playwrights with whom Dekker collaborated; and probably there were others. With nearly all of whom we know, he joined forces several times—for instance, in the late 1590's with Michael Drayton and in the 1620's with John Ford. Obviously, partnership with him must have been made easy by qualities like good temper and fairness. More significant, however, is the fact that as his earlier collaborators (whose association is known to us mostly through Henslowe's *Diary*) either died or retired from playmaking to other livelihoods, younger men like Middleton, Rowley, and Ford sought Dekker out or at least willingly entered into partnership with him for their own benefit. They saw advantage in his tutelage. Una Ellis-Fermor has remarked, "Everything he wrote could be played . . . most of it better than it can be read."[15] In the 1620's, no doubt, his craftsmanship must have been admired by writers who derided his old-fashioned themes and viewpoint.

As Miss Ellis-Fermor and others have observed, a successful collaboration resembles a chemical compound in that it may differ markedly from the plays created by the genius of the partners when each writes alone. Allowing for this undoubted fact, we still have to believe that Dekker's younger partners, as novices, made the lesser contribution; we must give Dekker major credit for the dramatic stamina of their joint plays. True, both Middleton and Ford possessed greater genius than Dekker. But without exception the best of his collaborations are those of which he wrote more than his share of the lines and apparently directed the composition. Two of these works, Part I of *The Honest Whore* and *The Witch of Edmonton,* rank high in Elizabethan drama.

CHAPTER 4

Dekker's Non-Dramatic Work

A S a writer of pamphlets, Dekker entered the field some twenty-five years after the publication of tracts had established itself as a profitable activity for stationers and authors and about eleven years after the full impact of Thomas Nashe's and Robert Greene's popularity had been felt in London.[1] Between Dekker's sixteenth and twenty-fourth years (1588–1596) most of Nashe's, Greene's, Thomas Lodge's, and Henry Chettle's tracts appeared, as well as the famous satiric ones in the Marprelate controversy. There were good reasons why any aspiring young writer might be fascinated with these pamphlets: They were cheap, they were topical, and their style revealed a sudden and stimulating improvement in popular prose, prose which had hitherto been confined to some kinds of religious controversy.[2] In sum, we may be puzzled by Dekker's tardiness in engaging in this writing until we recall that the theaters were also enjoying great prosperity from 1593 to 1603 and that acting companies were better paymasters than the stationers.

The evident reason why tracts were less remunerative for their authors than plays was that in setting the price of a book, the publisher seems to have used as his gauge the amount of paper required; he reckoned a penny a sheet in each copy.[3] On this basis, for a tract in quarto running to forty-eight pages, he would charge sixpence; and the whole edition of twelve hundred copies, if it sold out, would bring him thirty pounds. Out of the thirty pounds, of course, must be paid his own profit and the costs of the paper, printing, sewing, and distributing. To estimate the costs in detail is difficult and unnecessary; it is clear beyond doubt that only a few pounds could be spared to pay the author. Since we know that plays running in length to about eighty pages still sold for sixpence in Dekker's time, certainly other factors than just the cost of publication helped to determine their price. No doubt the popularity of plays in general and the names of individual playwrights made for rapid sales. However, we can see that the return of only thirty-five or forty pounds from the edition of a rather long tract would decidedly cut down profits, and we may therefore infer that publishers paid even less for tracts than actors were willing to pay for a play (usually six pounds). Hence, for the amount of time a writer had to invest in composition, he profited more from writing plays.

The term "tract" is now used to cover a variety of contents besides religious controversy in the pamphlets of Elizabethan England. "Social criticism" is perhaps not too philosophical a phrase to describe the denunciations made by Philip Stubbes, Stephen Gosson, and Barnabe Riche. Thomas Harman and Greene disclosed the knavery by which the underworld preyed on the honest; Anthony Munday exposed the Jesuits' machinations against England. Will Kemp wrote a news book about his own athletic exploits and it had the same appeal as the anonymous pamphlets that reported sensational murders, monstrous births, natural calamities, and military victories on the Continent. Sir John Harrington offered scatological humor. Chettle, Nashe, and Greene adapted medieval traditions of satire to war against Elizabethan vices.

Consequently, Dekker's casual reading for more than ten years had furnished him an abundance of models and styles when he decided, in 1603, to compose *The Wonderful Year* under the double impetus of relief that the succession had been settled peacefully and of anxiety at the fury of the plague—together with the extra pressure of financial need because of the closing of the theaters. He had encountered a great variety of techniques among the tracts: Frame-story, fantastic dream, dialogue, collections of anecdotes were common devices in such pieces as professed to be more than mere reports.

The years from 1603 to 1630 comprise the period during which appeared all the prose tracts, eighteen in all,[4] which scholars have thus far attributed to Dekker. To these may reasonably be added the "prison characters" he contributed to the collections going under the names of Sir Thomas Overbury and Geffray Mynshull, as well as two works in verse on topical subjects, *The Artillery Garden* and *Wars, Wars, Wars*. I shall also discuss two short religious poems, *Four Birds of Noah's Ark* and *Dekker's Dream*, in this chapter and thus broaden its scope to his non-dramatic works in general. For all of these works are aimed at the mass audience and belong to "popular" literature. The grand total, then, is about twenty-three distinct works. Of these I shall comment on eleven of the more representative and successful.

Classified by subjects, Dekker's non-dramatic works fall into six groups: the plague; national peril; social satire; swindles and cozening games; fiction; religion. The categories are not entirely logical or mutually exclusive, of course; for instance, the plague pamphlets, which are essentially reportage, also contain satiric invective against the cruelty of both city and country folk as well as religious exhortations to escape the wrath of God by amendment of evil ways. But the general purpose of any tract may be indicated well enough by one of the classifications. Approximately eight of the twenty-three titles fall in the class of satires and include such interesting ones as *The Seven Deadly Sins of London, A Knight's Conjuring, Lanthorn and Candlelight,*[5] *The Gull's Hornbook, Work for Armorers,* and *A Strange Horse Race*. The plague pamphlets total five, of which the best is *1603: The Wonderful Year;* the rest are quite inferior pieces. The two devotional works, *Four Birds* and *Dekker's Dream*, lack the intrinsic merit within their own genres which the satires mentioned have, although *Four Birds* has been praised for its style.

It would be hard to demonstrate, in fact, that Dekker finds any one of these purposes so much more congenial than others that any one of the classes by far excels the others in literary merit; nor is it true that Dekker's skill in writing prose increases remarkably through the years. Nevertheless, in this chapter I shall try to support two convictions: First, that Dekker found the traditions of satire, as adapted by Nashe and Greene, so apt to his temperament or so well exemplified by these writers that his best prose tracts are in this mode; and, second, that he shows a gradual improvement both in structure and style as the years pass. We may begin an appraisal of his tracts with the first one.

I *The Earlier Tracts, 1603–1612*

As *The Wonderful Year* was probably written during November, 1603, its account of the people's grief for Queen Elizabeth and their welcome of King James I is therefore a retrospection, written after seven months of terrors from the plague; hence it lacks the poignancy we should expect from Dekker's patriotic soul. Although Elizabeth's death had, of course, been long foreseen, the "nation [had been] almost begotten and borne vnder her . . . neuer sawe the face of any Prince but herself" during forty-five years (p. 12); consequently, one is disappointed with the frigidity of Dekker's rhetoric and his trite epigrams. Indeed, he had read too many funeral laments and afterwards seen too many horrid spectacles of the pestilence to recover the intensity of his grief in truly eloquent prose. King James was necessarily far less an inspiration than Elizabeth; the first third of the tract is, therefore, negligible.

The latter two-thirds, on the plague, is better; but it is still below any anticipations we may have formed by reading Daniel Defoe's *Journal*. Although the plague itself had been endemic in England for centuries, and although Nashe had given a precedent in *Christ's Tears over Jerusalem* (1593) for description of the horrors of starvation and disease, we may state without exaggeration that Dekker is here pioneering in the attempt to represent an uncontrollable national calamity. Aware of the magnitude of the task, he formally invokes Sorrow and Truth to lend him art "to delineate to the life the whole story of this mortall and pestiferous battaile" and to call up the ghosts of the dead to imprint their "ghastly vizages" on his paper (p. 26). Then he paints a nocturnal of stricken London, imaged first as a charnel house, next as a dwelling which is flaming around its trapped inmates.

About fifty-one lines have been devoted to these two vignettes. Now, in a dawn scene, the macabre fears of a rich man are pictured, even to his vision of burial in a pit with his enemies, where "the wormes that breed out of their putrifying carcasses, shall crawle in huge swarmes from them, and quite deuoure [him]" (p. 29). The worldling flees from London with his son, but the boy dies on the road; and the father, finding no one willing to touch the body, carries it home and buries it in his garden.

[*115*]

This powerful exemplum, occupying about eighty-seven lines, is probably taken from fact. Now Dekker lightens the tone and figures the pestilence as a motley army of which Death is the general; it besieges first the suburbs and then the city, whose denizens, if unable to flee, go "miching and muffled vp & downe with Rue and Wormewood stuft into their eares and nosthrils" to nullify infection. But some people profit from the calamity: Parish clerks, sextons, herb-sellers and gardeners prosper and pray for more business (pp. 31–35).

Next Dekker treats of those who have fled, many of them in vain; but even the healthy find themselves cruelly shunned by the "plough-driuers." Among the fugitives are the London physicians whose places in town are taken by quacks and mountebanks. Most miserable are victims dying of plague on the road, in the fields, or, if fortunate, in inns. And at this point, a little more than half way through the published tract, Dekker begins a series of anecdotes which comprise the remainder of the work. Nearly all are ironic, for the swiftness and unexpectedness of either death or recovery naturally lead to dramatic reversals. But Dekker lacks the control to give starkness and incisiveness to the irony; some sketches, in fact, are nearly ruined by verbosity. The best picture is one of the drunken tinker bellowing, "Haue ye any more Londoners to bury, hey downe a downe dery" (pp. 53–59). Rather abruptly, Dekker cuts off the series, having reached the manuscript equivalent of forty-eight printed pages; probably it was the limit the publishers had proposed.

My description has been so detailed to show that Dekker had a plan, which was (1) the death of Elizabeth, (2) the accession of James, (3) the horror of pestilence in the city, (4) the misery of the fugitives, and (5) illustrative anecdotes, many of them of grisly humor. But the parts really lack logical relationship, and, worse, Dekker's development of them lacks unification through tone or structure. Missing is a genuine unity of feeling and a climactic power. Rather obviously, the cause of failure is hasty composition. The appendix of anecdotes could go on indefinitely to illustrate the horror of the plague and to extend the book as needed. Only Nashe's verve of style can captivate a reader when the substance is so casual in method. Dekker's style in this tract is not worthy of comparison with that of Nashe.

After a lapse of three years, during which he had written several plays and two minor tracts, Dekker produced *The Seven Deadly Sins of London* (1606). If truly the work of one week, as the title page asserts with *Opus septem Dierum,* the structural idea was so clear that Dekker was able to concentrate entirely on expression; and the result decidedly excels *The Wonderful Year.* The plan is conventional: A pageant of the seven deadly sins enters London in triumph. The very familiar device, which Dekker had just used in *The Whore of Babylon,* perhaps made even a mere week's time sufficient for more deliberate composition and some revision, as well as for the writing of a pleasing dedication and an epistle. The epistle to the reader is excellent bait; it is exactly right in length and in its tone of jocular defiance:

> Reader, it is as ordinarie a custome (for vs that are Bookish) to haue a bout with thee, after wee haue done with a Patron, as for Schollers (in the noble science) to play at the woodden Rapier and Dagger at the ende of a Maisters prize. In doing which we know not vpon what Speeding points wee runne, for you (that are Readers) are the most desperate and fowlest players in the world, you will strike when a mans backe is towards you, and kill him (if you could for shame) when he lies vnder your feete.... You stand sometimes at a Stationers stal, looking scuruily (like Mules champing vpon Thistles) on the face of a new Booke bee it neuer so worthy: & goe (as il fauouredly) mewing away: But what get you by it? The Booke-seller euer after when you passe by, pinnes on your backes the badge of fooles to make you be laught to scorne, or of sillie Carpers to make you to be pittied: *Conradus Gesner* neuer writ of the nature of such strange beasts as you are. . . . I haue laide no blockes in thy way: if thou findest Strawes, *(Vale, vale,) caue ne titubes.* (pp. 5–6)

The following "Enterlude of Iniquitie" has an induction (preface), the latter half of which is an apostrophe to London. In effect, it is a recollection of *The Wonderful Year,* for it again cites the death of Elizabeth, the blessing of James's accession, and the fearful warning of the plague, now disregarded by sinful London. Thus it states the motivation of the tract: an admonition to the city that its vices must soon bring down again the wrath of God. The seven sins do not coincide exactly with the traditional cardinal ones[6]; Politic Bankruptism is a hybrid of

[*117*]

avarice and falsehood; Shaving is extortion, or avarice; Lying was not usually called a deadly sin by moralists; Candle-light hides a group of offenses, chiefly drunkenness and lechery; and Apishness is frivolous fashion—pride and waste. Sloth and Cruelty complete the seven. Taking waste as a species of sloth, we can see that, in Dekker's account of social offenses, inordinate love of money and wastefulness loom large; they are, in fact, the results of pride and the causes of cruelty. More than fifteen years of struggle against poverty must have shaped Dekker's view.

The satire, though at times caustic, is generally gay rather than bitter. Dekker ends the triumph of Sloth with the genial remark that "The Retayners that wear his cloth are *Anglers, Dumb Ministers, Players, Exchange-Wenches, Gamesters, Panders, Whores,* and *Fidlers.*" This manner is characteristic of the tract, less flamboyant than Nashe's, yet pleasantly ironic. The glimpses of Elizabethan life are lively, and there is little tedium. But what is to be said of the worth of the tract? Dekker lacks the power of Swift or Langland, of course, and no single, strong motif inspires the invective. But Dekker also has a more Christian wisdom than Swift; for he says that he will record these evils, "albeit they bee neuer reformed, till a second *Chaos* is to bee refined."[7] And his sincerity is unquestionable, even though his accusation has to be made in his own gentle style.

The tract was not reprinted, but probably sold well; it was followed in the same year by *News from Hell.* However, *News from Hell* was revised in 1607 and issued in a clearer and more complete version under the title *A Knight's Conjuring.* In both *Deadly Sins* and in *A Knight's Conjuring,* Dekker is complimenting Nashe by open imitation. Nashe's *Pierce Penniless's Supplication to the Devil* (1592) has a slight thread of narrative: Pierce the scholar-poet, having long experienced poverty, neglect, and "the spurns/That patient merit of the unworthy takes," writes his long supplication to Lucifer. He asks Lucifer to pay the rent he owes for the use of Pierce's empty purse, or else to take to Hell various kinds of sinners who are preempting Satan's powers in this world and monopolizing money in so doing. The satiric catalogue of these upstarts once again makes the portraits of the conventional seven deadly sins; but these are interspersed with manifold digressions, notably one denouncing

Gabriel Harvey and one eulogizing the English drama and the actors.

The supplication is accepted by a knight of the post (professional perjuror), a minor devil disguised, to be delivered to Lucifer. There follow a casual summary of demonology and an epistle to the reader which contains a eulogy of Spenser and an unnamed nobleman; then the tract abruptly ends. Nashe thought of writing the Devil's reply to Pierce, but never did so. An unknown writer published a sequel of no merit. Fourteen years later Dekker provided his sequel, recounting the journey of the knight of the post to Hell. But because Nashe's tract, although still remembered, was to many not so familiar in details as formerly, Dekker erred in assuming his readers would remember it as clearly as he did. *News from Hell* opens very obscurely for one who has forgotten about Nashe's unimportant knight of the post. In *A Knight's Conjuring*, Dekker tried, not quite successfully, to clarify the exposition; for some reason he also omitted a fine invocation of "fluent, facetious" Thomas Nashe that he had introduced in *News from Hell*. At the end of *News*, the knight goes to Elysium to report to Nashe the failure of his application; in *Conjuring*, this interview is more appropriately held on the infernal shore to which Nashe is brought temporarily for the purpose. And in *Conjuring*, abandoning the knight's point of view, Dekker describes Elysium with even more sentimental detail and with some humor.

In their common substance, *News* and *Conjuring* resemble *Pierce* in loose structure and in lively humor; and they are not much below *Pierce* in vivacity of style. We miss the incomparable egoism of Nashe, of course; and we are not quite compensated by Dekker's sincere but conventional touches of religious piety. Nashe oscillates between his own point of view and Pierce's; but, since these coincide morally, unity of tone is not really violated.[8] In contrast, the views of Dekker and the knight of the post are not at all identical, and the shift between them is more awkward. Yet there are some excellent passages in the knight's journey, especially the dispute between Charon and Mercury over some unpaid accounts—evidently imitated from a Thames wherryman's argument with a customer.[9] In contrast to Nashe, Dekker satirizes players and sympathizes with soldiers.

Both writers believe that the further "enlargement of Gold," (affluence for the poet) is impossible so long as Plutus is blind and vice continues to reign in society.[10]

Structurally, *The Seven Deadly Sins* is superior to *News* and *Conjuring*. They present a gallimaufry: short sermons on death, Heaven, and Hell; allegory in the significance of Hell's rivers; eulogy of an English captain in Elysium; satire on vice, perversity, and delusion; and the farce of Mercury and Charon. The tone varies between indignation, facetiousness, and sentiment. The variation has at the same time a personal quality and a conventionality, both borrowed from Nashe. Dekker felt quite at home in this kind of work.

In *The Bellman of London* (1608) Dekker turned back, obviously, to earlier models than Nashe—to John Awdeley, Harman, and Greene, in their exposés of thieves and cozeners.[11] Here again his idea was sound. The older tracts had been partly forgotten, or at least not reprinted sufficiently for the demand; and in Dekker's superior redaction their contents proved very popular; *The Bellman* reached five editions by 1640. It is a more orderly exposition than his preceding ones except *Seven Deadly Sins,* and it is written with some care and precision, and with the expressed hope that its reception will warrant a sequel. Although the narrative basis is implausible and illogical, Dekker's moral indignation is genuine and strong. Certainly he sees the humor in some of the tricks he describes, but he does not annoy the reader by the obvious duplicity of denouncing cleverness in which he really takes delight. Stylistically, *The Bellman* pleases by its straightforwardness and freedom from mannerisms such as the silly vestige of euphuism in Greene's prose.

Lacking royalties from the successive editions,[12] Dekker had no alternative but to write the promised sequel, *Lanthorn and Candlelight, or the Bellman's Second Night's Walk* (1608). If the continuations and revisions of *Lanthorn* as *O per se O, Villainies Discovered,* and *English Villainies* are considered as essentially the same work, *Lanthorn* proved even more popular than *The Bellman* and was published in at least nine editions by 1648. The attention drawn to *Bellman* led Dekker to equip *Lanthorn* with a full apparatus of Latin marginal notes, a dedicatory epistle to Master Francis Mustian, an epistle to "my owne

Nation," and three complimentary poems by John Day,[13] Matthew Royden, and Edward Grimeston. Though biographical information about all three is scarce, Day and Royden seem to have been of Dekker's own generation; and the absence of a younger satirist like Hall or Marston indicates both the nature of Dekker's friendships and his purpose in this unusually long tract. He is presenting himself seriously as a moralist as he has done implicitly in most of his dramas. Considering the literary ethics of that age, to recognize his plagiarism from Harman and Greene does not impugn his sincerity.

Though we may smile at the introductory device of going back to Babel to account for the rogues' cant which is the chief interest of the book, the structure is carefully planned. We are shown another council in Hell and an emissary who is despatched to Earth to spread vice among more respectable classes—because the supply of rogues has been cut off by the success of *The Bellman!* The emissary meets the Bellman in the dark, takes him for a fellow-devil, and foolishly reveals all the villainies he has discovered and inspired. The various forms of swindling are managed by disreputable persons in a social range from horse-traders to avaricious merchants. In spite of touches of humor, the tone and style are soberer than in any tract since *The Wonderful Year*. Nashe's exuberance can be detected only occasionally in the style.

A recent critic remarks about Dekker in these two tracts that "His chief additions to underworld literature were his graphic jargon and his interesting framework for his material."[14] True, these booklets have little originality; Dekker principally collected and modernized the rogue lore of his predecessors. But it would be a blunder to deny either his serious purpose or an actual good effect from the widespread interest in the tracts.[15]

After producing a third tract in 1608, *The Dead Term,* an inferior piece in the shape of a moral dialogue between the cities of Westminster and London, Dekker published in 1609 his now best-known work in prose, *The Gull's Hornbook*. Its popularity in our age, however, arises from causes which did not affect Jacobean readers to the same extent: its pictures of the walk in St. Paul's, the ordinaries, and the theaters as the resorts of idle young men. Especially because of our intense interest in

Shakespeare's theater, what seemed to Dekker's audience a mildly amusing view of the commonplace has become a vital document. *The Gull's Hornbook* was never reprinted as Dekker's,[16] and no allusions suggest that it created much interest. That it was a comparative failure in 1609 would not, of course, diminish its lasting merits as description. But, even for the modern reader, Dekker's basic conception lacks full validity.

The author almost confesses as much "To the Reader": "[*The book*] *hath a relish of* Grobianisme, *and tastes very strongly of it in the beginning.*" That is to say, Dekker begins with an imitation of Friedrich Dedekind's *Grobianus,* consisting of instructions on how to be a sloven and a boor. But as C. H. Herford observes, this satiric attack on gross manners, which had point for German society, did not strike home in England. There, if satiric comedy of the time is an indication, the "fop, the rusty scholar, and the misanthrope, were the most available equivalents" for Grobian (let us add the usurious merchant and his lewd wife to the list).[17] Gradually perceiving the inappropriateness of his theme, Dekker shifts to a satire on the fop—as he says, "*of a Dutchman fashioned a meere Englishman*"—but "between the two characters the whole book fluctuates awkwardly enough."[18] Naturally, the change of purpose increases the heaviness of the basic irony, particularly in the earlier chapters in which exaggeration is most obvious.

Although Dekker does not present a perfectly chronological account of the gull's daily round of activities, the tract has more simplicity and clarity than several of its predecessors. We find some vestiges of the traditional freedom to digress that characterizes popular satire; but, on the whole, the description moves forward at a steady pace. By 1609 Dekker is master of an easy, varied sentence style and of diction spiced with facetiousness and irony. A typical passage gives directions for the gull's visit to St. Paul's cathedral:

... The first time that you venture into Powles, passe through the body of the Church like a Porter, yet presume not to fetch so much as one whole turne in the middle Ile, no nor to cast an eye to *Si quis* doore, (pasted and plaistered vp with Seruing-mens *supplications*) before you haue paid tribute to the top of *Powles* steeple with a single penny: And when you are mounted there, take heede how you looke downe into the yard; for the railes are as rotten as your great-Grandfather; and thereupon it will not be amisse if you enquire how *Kit Woodroffe* durst vault ouer, and what reason he had for it, to put his necke in hazard of reparations. From hence you may descend, to talke about the horse that went vp, and striue, if you can, to know his keeper: take the day of the Moneth, and the number of the steppes, and suffer yourselfe to belieue verily it was not a horse, but something else in the likenesse of one: which wonders you may publish, when you returne into the country, to the great amazement of all Farmers Daughters, that will almost swound at the report, and neuer recouer till their banes bee asked twice in the Church.

Stylistically, *The Gull's Hornbook* is not so pungent as *Knight's Conjuring*, but it makes very pleasant reading. For the student of English literature, *The Hornbook* provides most useful and entertaining vignettes of everyday life in Jacobean London.

Work for Armorers (1609) perhaps even improves on the vivacious prose that delights us in *The Gull's Hornbook*. In satiric allegory, *Work for Armorers* tells of a war between Poverty and Riches which ends in a stalemate. Although the social groups and evils chosen for satire are the familiar subjects of sixteenth-century homilies and invectives, Dekker avoids tedium by clarity of structure and by judiciously rapid handling of the traditional ideas in a tone of genial irony, which, however, sometimes verges on the caustic. On the other hand, since Dekker is never adept at contriving a lively opening for a prose narrative, the beginning of *Work for Armorers* is indirect and unclear. First comes the speaker's personal reminiscence of frustration, boredom, and poverty; then suddenly the contest between Money and Poverty begins. Moreover, the war ends too abruptly because Dekker can conceive of no real solution of the problem on the terms in which he views it. Yet for a study of Dekker's social and economic ideas, none of his tracts is more illuminating and readable, in spite of our feeling of disappointment at the indecisiveness of the conclusion and at Dekker's resignation, bordering on cynicism—a disappointment which results from the difference between his social outlook and our own, a difference I shall return to in Chapter 5.

If we omit the very inferior *Raven's Almanac*, a mock-prognostication (which was probably the first of the four tracts pub-

lished in 1609[19]), then the last work Dekker issued in that year
is his first book of devotion[20]—the prose *Four Birds of Noah's
Ark.* He uses the conventional symbolism of the birds with but
little modification for his purposes, indeed, for more specious
division of the kinds of prayer than is artistically needed, not to
say required by logic. The dove, emblem of innocence, lends its
nature to prayers suitable to the "yong & the meanest people";
the eagle, of vision, soars with prayers for rulers and public oc-
casions; the pelican, of spiritual health in Christ, inspires to
prayers against the seven deadly sins; and the phoenix, of life,
fosters meditation on the five mysteries of Christ's mission—His
death, burial, resurrection, ascension, and coming in glory. In
effect, the divisions are these: Part I: domestic and vocational
prayers fitted for one's station in life, for the farmer, mariner,
mariner in peril, merchant, wife in pregnancy, midwife, and the
like; Part II: prayers on behalf of rulers, the various social
classes and officials, as well as supplications in time of war, pestilence, famine, and so on; Part III: universal prayers against the
cardinal sins; and Part IV: meditations on the Lord's triumph—
in effect, universal prayers.

The reader will do well to begin with parts III and IV since
I and II serve largely as homilies, preachments on the duties
of one's state. The first sentence of Part I will serve to illustrate
the instructive tone carried to a degree of unnaturalness in such
prayer. It begins a prayer for "a childe before he goeth to his
study, or to schoole" and reads: "O God, that are the fountaine
of all wisdome, & founder of all learning: breathe into my soule
the spirit of understanding, that in my childhood I may learne,
and (as I grow farther into yeres) may practise the study only
of thee and of thy lawes." In short, it is mainly a preachment
to the child, not his own utterance to his God.

But in parts III and IV Dekker, speaking by and for himself,
offers thought that is sound, simple, and sincere. His prayers are
not marked by deep insight or passion. They repeat the simple
notes of a virtuous soul, unenclined by nature to mysticism and
limited in devotional reading by the demands of making a
meager living for his family. These meditations, in short, are
not comparable to Thomas à Kempis's or Blaise Pascal's. They
speak no truths which pierce as they enlighten us, none even

so poignant as one or two to be found in his appendix to the book, "Short and pithie Sentences, fit to be applied to those purposes, for which the former Prayers were made." The sentences are taken from a compendium of aphorisms of the Fathers, *Flores Doctorum,* which gave Dekker the texture of his prayers.[21] But *Birds of Noah's Ark* gives us the sincere, natural piety of a loyal Anglican in Elizabeth's age, for our better understanding of that generation; and possibly for some readers there may be spiritual value, not just the historical.

Between 1609 and 1613 (the year in which the seven years' imprisonment began) occurred a dearth of publication and of other signs of Dekker's activity which has already been noted in Chapter I. Certainly we can infer that he returned to play writing, but we have to conclude that even the titles of most of the plays have been lost or assigned to other dates. Of tracts there is only *A Strange Horse-Race* (entered in the Stationers' Register on January 21, 1613). Compared with the pamphlets of 1607–1609, it is quite inferior. Indeed, it seems to me a plausible guess that *Horse-Race* must have been first drafted ten or more years before, perhaps in the late 1590's. In substance it is another combination of fantasy and satire, much in the manner of *Pierce Penniless;* but this medley is burdened with pedantical learning borrowed, probably, from compendia or handbooks of history. More precisely, pedantry clogs the first of three minor tracts very possibly written independently and later glued together, as it were, by some degree of revision: *A Strange Horse-Race, The Catchpolls' Masque,* and *The Bankrouts' Banquet.* The last two are skits, fantasies of Hell and its occupants, a subject that we have seen Dekker returning to repeatedly, largely under the inspiration of Nashe. They do not profess to teach, and they draw from the writer's earlier, not his more recent, reading. The style of all three, however, appears uniform enough to suggest approximately the same years of origin—the period before Dekker had learned the greater sophistication to be seen in *A Knight's Conjuring,* for instance.

"A Moral Labyrinth," Dekker calls the book; but he may have had in mind chiefly the first section, *Horse-Race.* In it he preposterously aims to trace a warfare, or universal conflict, first in the realms of man's own races (specifically, Roman races, amphitheatrical contests, and triumphs); next among the celestial bodies; then among the natural elements (represented in alchemical terms and theories); and, finally and at greatest length, among the virtues and vices—and this section gives opportunity for traditional satiric sketches of embodiments of vice. We may dignify this philosophical olio by saying that Dekker may have intended to represent figuratively that principle in the concept of the Great Chain of Being by which every level of being is urged upward toward the next highest, and every form leans toward the greater excellence of the one above it. But Dekker's thinking is obscure, perhaps confused. For instance, morally speaking, the contrast between niggardliness and liberality lies in the object desired (material goods in the one case; love, in the other) —not in an essential difference of spiritual action. The soul, though aware of the higher good, attaches itself to the lower one; and hence a disturbance occurs in the spirit and a so-called conflict between vice and virtue. But two different directions of desire are not two forms of being. Dekker's attempt to use the principle of being that aspires to higher forms is basically irrational. That it was his intention to use the principle is clearly indicated, I think, by the aspirations he attributes to the elements in the third exemplum, for instance, in which tin aspires to become silver.

The social satire in this first section lacks pungency and vividness equal to that in *Seven Deadly Sins* and in *Lantern and Candlelight,* even though the style is more disciplined than in *The Catchpolls' Masque* and in *The Bankrouts' Banquet.* These parts were perhaps written earlier. In brief, the *Masque* tells that "The Grand-Sophy of the Satanicall Synagogue," hearing from Fame that he is losing the battle with Virtue for human souls, falls into such a passion of rage that he fears his own death and makes his will in which he bequeaths appropriate souvenirs to London's sinners—a fairly lively piece of Nashean satire.[22] But the "Tartarian Termagant" then recovers and orders a replenishment of his troops by new births in Hell. The fresh spawn of demons include, notably, Hypocrisy and Ingratitude, whose effects in England are then described at length.

Other offspring of Hell are Schism, Atheism, Paganism, Idiotism, Apostacy, Impenitency, Diffidence, Presumption, "and a whole generation of such others." To celebrate these births, the catchpolls' masque is presented to the "upsitters" at the christening! But the masque is only briefly described, and a final passage of medieval satire attacks the catchpolls of this world, who include all the avaricious: "Any one that takes Bribes, and holds the Scale of Iustice with an vn-even hand, laying the rich mans cause (be it neuer so bad) in the heauy scale, and the poore mans (be it neuer so good) in the light one, hee is a *Catchpoll*."[23]

Finally, *The Bankrouts' Banquet* is a feeble piece of satiric fantasy in law-terms; the sweetmeats consist of legal instruments: bonds, defeasances, attachments, etc. The section ends with an invective against deliberate bankrupts who thus defraud their neighbors. Like *The Catchpolls' Masque, The Banquet* has a good deal of passable imitation of Nashe's volubility. Although the description of the contents on the title page of the tract is somewhat inaccurate, the Latin motto and the spelling "Dekker" may indicate the dramatist's own preparation of the copy for the printer. He also provided a dedicatory epistle and a note to the "understanders"; hence we may infer that in 1613 either he was not conscious of the inferiority of his work or he was well aware that his name increased its saleability.

II *Later Works in Prose and Verse*

Almost seven years' confinement in King's Bench Prison, 1613–1619, led very naturally to the publication of *Dekker's Dream,* dated 1620.[24] It is his somber meditation on the Three Last Things; there is scarcely a glimpse of Heaven—in fact, Death hardly figures either; the subjects really are the Last Judgment and Hell. In his epistle to the young courtier, Endymion Porter, friend to Prince Charles, Dekker writes in the contemporary Senecan style: "There is a Hell named in our Creede, and a Heauen, and the Hell comes before: If we looke not into the first, we shall neuer liue in the last."[25] There we see the purpose of the tract: It is a homily. It calls up for us the terrible signs before the Doomsday, the awful coming of Christ the Judge, and the rising of the dead. Dekker briefly interpolates an ecstatic, generalized description of Heaven; then he resumes his account of the Judgment and the sentencing. There follows a long description of Hell, which mingles Classical, Biblical, and medieval elements in its imagery of the topography of the region and of its denizens, its rulers, and the punishments of the damned. A sinner's voice, which reproaches God for these unendurable punishments, is properly answered by a voice defending his justice. Dekker awakes.

Although the greatest part of the tract is in decasyllabic couplets, there are several prose passages commenting on the method, defending the use of pagan mythological material, and indicating the Biblical sources. Abundant marginal notes multiply the citations of authority, identify persons and events, and partition the contents of the work. Apparently *Dekker's Dream* is designed for young as well as old; it is to be a book for family piety. The couplets have the same fluency which characterizes the poet's blank verse in drama. On the awful scene of the resurrection of the dead on the last day he writes:

> That Lord, by his Owne Subiects Crucified,
> Lo, at this Grand Assize comes Glorified,
> With troopes of Angels, who his Officers are,
> To call by sound of Trumpe his Foes to a Bar
>
> . . . . .
>
> Arm'd (Cap-a-pe) thus, who 'gainst him durst fight?
> There was no ground for Strength, nor yet for Flight.
> At this (me thought) All Graues that euer held
> Dead Coarses, yawn'd wide-open, and compell'd
> The bones of Dead-men vp with Flesh to rise;
> Yea, those on whom the Seas did tyrannize,
> And droun'd in wrackes, and which were peece-meale eaten,
> With liuely bodies to the shoares were beaten;
> Whom Sword, or Fire, Iibbets, or Wheeles had torne,
> Had their own limbes againe, and new were borne;
> From the first Man God made, to the last that died,
> The Names of All, were here Examplified....[26]

Although there are a few passages which, like the preceding, claim our attention by their poetic feeling, Dekker's vision of Hell is so surpassed by Milton's that we are conscious of a little embarrassment. Dekker's poem, of course, is an attempt to adapt the medieval dream vision to his own times, and he does his

[*128*]

best to dignify it with proper classical trappings in the Renais-sance manner. His sincerity and his touches of pathos and awe create some appeal; but the weary writer lacked the genius, the time, and the vigor to make a work of art. And he lacked, or at least he did not find, a model to follow.

After the *Dream,* Dekker composed about six more tracts,[27] five of them published in three years, 1628–1630. Three of the six are plague pamphlets first reprinted and claimed for Dekker by the late F. P. Wilson: *A Rod for Runaways; London, Look Back;* and *The Black Rod and the White Rod.* In pattern these three much resemble his earlier tracts on the theme; but the homiletic note is more insistent, for the religious feeling of an old, world-weary man overrides his interest in the ironic, ma-cabre, and tragic events already too familiar to him. In style and organization they are less coherent and impressive than his earlier work.

Possibly the most interesting of the six tracts is *Penny-Wise, Pound-Foolish,* Dekker's only known venture into the field of the *novella.* The moral tale of a young merchant's infidelity to his wife and his punishment for it presents us with figures famil-iar from Dekker's plays: the wife, as Griselda, putting up with all wrongs; the impudent but kind London courtesan; the shrewd, generous, faithful servant (in this instance, personified in a sailor of the merchant's crew). Though very readable, the tale mani-fests no superiority to most such pieces in its time. Ferdinand's first infidelity, that with the London courtesan, is motivated in quite a perfunctory way; his second straying comes from his al-ready demonstrated sensuality and from the conventionally over-whelming allure of Venetian *bona robas.*[28] The patient wife, Annabell, more incredible in this story than in Dekker's plays, never once utters a reproach. Instead of a St. Christopher medal or an Agnus Dei, this Protestant Griselda gives her adventurous husband a penny, for which he is to bring her a good return on her investment. The penny, given by Ferdinand to the faithful sailor Theobald, becomes the symbol of Annabell's devotion and Ferdinand's sin, the peg from which the tale hangs and derives its title. Theobald's honesty and generosity restore the bank-rupt Ferdinand to middle-class comfort at the end. Although less realistic than Defoe's novels, the fiction is much in his manner. Moll Flanders's repentance and prosperity come to mind at once.

Perhaps the narrative technique is a little worsened by Dekker's training in the theater, where the dull conventionalism of the affair with the London courtesan and the feeble business of Ferdinand's attack on the Italian grandee's man-servant in the dark would be carried off well enough by the actors' skill, a skill, incidentally also needed for the disguised Ferdinand's tricking the London courtesan out of the jewels he has formerly given her. Of course, Dekker had few models of real merit to teach him better fictional technique. And his style does not suggest hasty or casual composition. Approximately the first half of the thirty-nine pages of the tale are written in conventionally florid style marked by Latinized diction, careful balance and suspense in the sentence, ostentatious metaphors, and alliteration:

But after his cogitation had thus ranne [!] diuision on her praises, his Vnderstanding began to fall into another tune, and his Memory to be set to this Note, to call to minde his dear and disconsolate *Annabell* in *Bristow;* presenting her therefore to his Remembrance, and the full volume of all her Vertues, being printed in his soule, he thus brake forth into a passionate reprehension of his new conceited folly.[29]

But this artifice is never obtrusive, and about midway it gradually disappears altogether, being replaced by Dekker's good, workaday prose, with its more colloquial structure and its diction and figures drawn from familiar life, including his nautical experience.

Dekker's name does not appear on the title page, nor is it affixed to the "Epistle to the Reader" or the discourse on "The Excellent Worth of a Penny" which make up the preliminaries, sheet A; but its absence does not argue his indifference to the tract.

III *Evaluation*

In evaluating Dekker's accomplishment in his non-dramatic work, loosely gathered under the heading of "tracts," we must admit that, as a satirist, he is sincere, but imitative, conventional, and uneven. He becomes too homiletic and hortatory, then drops into the merely facetious. For his sincerity a passage in *The Whore of Babylon* (1606) may be taken as significant. Using physicians and surgeons figuratively for the divines and satirists who profess to heal England's diseases, Dekker says that these healers must first cleanse their own corruption and that the satirists especially "rip vp the bowels of vice in such a beastly manner, that . . . the beholders learn more villany then they knew before. . . . "[30] He avoids the mask of the ironist, perhaps mainly because of the prevalent conception of the satyr-satirist,[31] notably exemplified by Marston; for Dekker found it morally ambiguous. He adheres, instead, to the medieval method of the social survey, but he focusses upon London and its classes. For this reason he appears anachronistic and insipid compared to Jonson, Marston, and their school (though, no doubt, much more so to us than to his own generation). Yet Dekker surprises us by his constant faith in the worth of his writings, a faith grounded in his steady allegiance to such elemental virtues as piety, charity, and humility. While, admittedly, his forthright devotion to Christian virtue was incongruous with the contemporary fashion in satire, yet it was basic in late medieval satire.

If we take the term "realism" to denote a vivid depiction of manners through the use of racy, colloquial language, then, in his prose, Dekker is a realist who merits comparison with Nashe and Greene. Dekker's realism, however, is essentially an auxiliary to exhortation and denunciation. His fictions (apart from *Penny-Wise, Pound-Foolish*) are merely anecdotes or sketches subserving another purpose; they are either *exempla* of vice and virtue or simply entertainment. Perhaps *The Gull's Hornbook* has exaggerated critics' impressions of Dekker's realism. As a criterion for judging his artistry, realism has a distinctly subordinate importance. We are left, I think, to judge the success of Dekker's moralistic prose on the basis of the effectiveness of its technique—its structure and style.

As has been noted in speaking of particular tracts, Dekker's structure is often tentative or clumsy, rarely firm and clear. He may change his purpose midway (as in *The Gull's Hornbook*), expand an episode more or less whimsically (*A Knight's Conjuring*), or trail off in a series of anecdotes without climax (the plague pamphlets). In style, however, he is nearly always clear, vivacious, racy, and free from affectation. When we read *Work for Armorers,* for instance, we may regret that Dekker did not try really to emulate Thomas Nashe and Thomas Deloney in the short novel or Joseph Hall and Sir Thomas Overbury in character-writing.[32] Whatever his reasons, Dekker confined himself practically to the amorphous journalistic tract. As a journalist, he displays little originality; he does not intend surprise or novelty in content or style in order to capture his audience. Rather, he is essentially a moralist who uses topical subjects because of their interest or urgency. He can ignore mere novelty in expression or viewpoint, yet succeed on his merits as a sincere, humorous writer with a fine, colloquial style.

CHAPTER 5

Dekker's Religious and Social Thought

PRIMARILY as a successful writer of tracts, secondarily as dramatist of a conservative kind, Dekker becomes important in literary history for his expression of the religious and social outlook of a large segment, perhaps the majority, of the Elizabethan public. Because that age was one of religious controversy and accelerating social change manifested in ideologies as diverse as those of John Foxe, Calvinist, Christopher Marlowe, infidel, and Robert Parsons, Catholic, Dekker's views are valuable, not for their novelty, but for their typicality and for the assumptions on which they rest. Yet his statements are not connected, systematic exposition. For this reason a synthesis of his ideas is appropriate.

I *Religion*

From occasional comments in the preceding chapters on the plays and tracts, it has become clear that, in religion, Dekker appears to be a very orthodox Anglican. As we have seen in Chapter 1, the two indictments for recusancy brought against him in his last years originated, no doubt, in his absence from church on Sunday because of fear of arrest for debt. In Elizabethan and Jacobean times, heterodoxy invariably drew the attention of the authorities and left traces in public records. This was the result for Marlowe, Thomas Kyd, Ben Jonson, and George Chapman, and we must infer that it would have been so for Shakespeare, Thomas Middleton, and Dekker had they not maintained conformity with the Established Church. This evidence, although negative, has significance.

Similarly, if we stop to reflect on Dekker's deeply religious nature, his general avoidance of controversial religious topics has more meaning than at first appears. Indeed, in this light the negative assumes positive value. Nowhere in two religious works —*The Four Birds of Noah's Ark* and *Dekker's Dream*—nor, of course, elsewhere, does he touch on points of doctrine or liturgy that were sensitive in that age of conflict. For instance, he says nothing about the sacrament of the Lord's Supper, prayer for the dead, or the authority of bishops. Although in *If This Be Not a Good Play* we can read signs of an uncommon respect for religious orders and celibacy, Dekker is quite the Protestant Englishman in his attitude toward the assumed tyranny and corruption of the Papacy. His references to his own Church and its hierarchy are few, except for the patriotic ones in *The Whore of Babylon*. The only comment which sounds a critical note is made in *If This Be Not a Good Play*, and Naples, the distant setting of the story, muffles the application to England in 1611. Learning of King Alphonso's confiscation of his priory, Friar Clement says, "Woe to those dayes,/When to raise Vpstarts, the poore CHVRCH decayes/.... I feare RELIGIONS Fall" (III.3. 122–123, 134). In his plague pamphlets, Dekker nowhere, I believe, mentions any heroic devotion of pastors to their flocks. He once remarks, "... many Physicians of our soules flye the City, and their sicke Patients want those heavenly medicines which they are tyed to giue them, & those that stay by it, stand aloofe."[1] But his general silence on the faults of the Church indicates a predominant loyalty and wish to avoid giving her enemies any opening for attack.

A description of the tenets of Dekker's faith must, therefore, be largely inferential and, for its conclusions, draw chiefly on what is more definite than his creed, namely, his personality. In youth, his compassionate nature presumably caused him to reject (if he encountered it) the more austere form of Calvinism as too harsh and repugnant, and his loyalty to queen and country automatically aroused his opposition to Brownist, Anabaptist, and Presbyterian plans of church government as opposed to the Anglican. Dekker ranks Precisians (puritan reformers) with Turks and Jews as objects of contempt, and his references to "the sober *Perpetuana* suited Puritane" show the rancor that is usual among dramatists.

A few critics have described Dekker as a Puritan, presumably because of his intimate knowledge of the Bible and his moralistic tone. But he was not a Puritan in any proper sense of that term. Miss Kate L. Gregg concludes, after citing examples of Dekker's antipathy to Puritans, that when he thought about religion and the state, he was an Anglican; when he spoke of abuses in the Church, he was a Puritan; and when he considered the relations of God and man, he was a Calvinist. " ... As a Calvinist [he] emphasized the omnipotence of God, the depravity of man, the need for repentance, the marvels of God's grace. ... " Possibly two fallacies underly these remarks: One assumes that anyone who was outspokenly critical of faults in the Anglican clergy should be termed "Puritan," surely a mistaken conception; the other assumes that Anglicans were unconcerned about "the omnipotence of God," and so on. Dekker was as orthodox a member of the Church of England as Edmund Spenser or John Donne.[2]

We may reasonably suppose that Dekker accepted uncritically the doctrines preached in the parish churches he attended in his youth and manhood, and that the ministers happened to be thorough believers in what was later called the "Middle Way." True, Dekker is outspoken on the necessity of good works conjoined with faith, but he alludes figuratively to these two means of salvation as wings and does not pretend to settle any theological dispute: "Exercise both, and be sure thou shalt get thither [to Heaven]." He has a deep reverence for the Bible, "that Booke where no untruthes can be read"; he probably read it as much as most religious men do in their youth, and he devoted himself to reading the Bible during his long imprisonment (as *Dekker's Dream* testifies) and in his last years.[3] In neither the insistence on good works nor the Bible-reading was he unusual among Anglicans. No doubt *Dekker's Dream* evidences truly enough his humble acceptance of the basic doctrines of the Anglican faith about the Fall of Man and the Redemption. Dekker's mind, I believe, was not the sort that constantly tries to refine and strengthen its beliefs by analysis and test. Temperamentally, he was much more like Thomas à Kempis in preferring to feel compunction rather than to be able to define it.

Yet in that comparison we perhaps praise him too highly. In Part I of *The Honest Whore,* in describing the effects of sin,

Dekker dwells almost entirely on such worldly punishments as disease, ostracism, and poverty—not on the spiritual punishments of isolation, self-loathing, and remorse; and he speaks very little even of the terrors of the Judgment Day. But we must grant that the worldly consequences are more easily pictured for the imagination of a theater audience, and that—when he is using the medium of the tracts—the topicalities with which he generally deals call for the devices of irony or invective more than for meditation and spiritual analysis. Making every allowance for the pressure under which he had to write, the fact remains that Dekker has left us no poignant passages of spiritual insight and no tragedy worthy of the name. Deep religious feeling is perhaps but one source of great literary insight and power, even in a writer like Tolstoy; and Dekker's failure to achieve greatness should not be attributed solely to his kind of religiosity. However, in conclusion, his religion may fairly be described as sentimental if we mean by the term that his literary work presents a conventional, commonplace interpretation of man's feelings about God and the supernatural life.

II *View of Society*

As orthodox as his religious sentiments is Dekker's view of social evil and natural catastrophe. Our dissatisfaction with the moralizing in the plague pamphlets (we also feel it, but somewhat less, with the satires, like *The Seven Deadly Sins*) may be due too much to our twentieth-century sociological attitudes which have not fully proved their superiority to Dekker's principles. Yet even today a man who professes firm religious convictions, and, therefore, a somewhat supernatural and mystical view of evils like the plague (or cancer) wishes that Dekker were not so simplistic in his explanation of the cause of the epidemic. And any other type of modern reader will merely dismiss Dekker as "medieval." But as Professor Wilson observes, the supernatural explanation of plague was the prevailing one, even among medical writers like Thomas Vicary, not to speak of spiritual ones like John Donne and John Bunyan.[4] We have to admit that for Dekker's audience a fuller rationalizing of the theological ideas was assumed to be unnecessary or was to be more properly left to be made by the preachers. Dekker can say without any thought of dissent: "And shall I tell you why these Feares are come amongst vs? Looke vpon the Weapon which hath struck other Nations; and the same Arme that wounded them, smites now at vs, and for the same quarrell (*Sinne*)."[5] By this statement of fundamental truth, Dekker does not, of course, deny the mediation of physical agents like tainted air, which carry the plague and which in individual cases may be counteracted or avoided. He asserts only that Providence has chosen to concentrate in London the occult physical sources of the disease.

In contrast to disease, war stems obviously from man's will when it has been subjugated by pride and greed. Dekker's remarks on war display more inconsistency than those of some of his contemporaries, Shakespeare, for instance. On the one hand, all during his life Dekker was thrilled by war's panoply; no Elizabethan was more the victim of kettle-drums. At about the age of fifty-six he writes that his heart "danceth sprightly, when I see/ (Old as I am) our *English Gallantry*," meaning the London militia, or trained bands, on parade. "To see three thousand men together in Armour in a field, is a goodly sight...."[6] On the other hand, he knows that "continuall wars are continuall slaueries."[7] He probably saw no inconsistency in his position.

In *Wars, Wars, Wars,* Dekker eulogizes his subject by reciting, in a succession of figures, the commonplace arguments in favor of war: It is the school of honor and arms; it brings home spoils for the commonwealth; it dissipates the pressures of ambition and sedition; it heightens morale in the state; it heals the cankers of a long peace (such as pride at court, simony, bribery, usury, and fraud), and it lops off the unfruitful members of society that "steale away the Sap from the profitable boughes of a King-dome."[8] But most of these ideas are expressed in metaphors; I do not know that Dekker anywhere writes a cogently reasoned, philosophical defense of war.

With respect to the suffering caused by war, Dekker confines himself almost entirely to the misery of the soldiers on their campaigns and after their discharge. Their endurance of bad diet, exposure, and vermin or their pawning of clothing for drink (while their captains live high on dead pay) and their beggary after returning to England—these are his themes: "The Souldier[']s staruing at the doore/Ragd, leane, and pale through

[*137*]

want of blood,/Sold cheape by him for Countries good."[9] Of the suffering of civilians and the waste of national resources Dekker does not speak. Nor does his admiration for patriotic heroism compensate us for this omission, which is most easily (but not necessarily truly) explained by the supposition that he had never seen actual warfare.

With regard to economic problems, Dekker's thought is generally in the medieval tradition. The writers who acted as pioneers for Mercantilist doctrine—the new "money economy" associated with growing European nationalism—were beginning to influence English thought; but it is doubtful that Dekker ever seriously read on economic theory or knew the ideas of such theorists as Niccolo Machiavelli and Jean Bodin at all well.[10] Perhaps the only notable principle of Mercantilism that is discernible in Dekker's tracts is his exaltation of the importance of money, by which he makes it the chief treasure of a state, practically identifying it with wealth. Whence he drew this conception it is hard to say. Less definitely suggestive of the new theory are his constant denunciations of waste and wastrels and of "politic bankruptism." On the other hand, he does not glorify foreign trade or place manufacturing above agriculture in importance.

In Mercantilist theory abundant population leads to national wealth by supplying a labor force at subsistence level and by making colonies feasible. But Dekker is so little concerned for increase of population that he attributes to the plague the benefit of removing a surplus! Although he often dedicates his books to businessmen (if this fact could be said to show his admiration for commerce), against it must be set his elaborate portrayal of Bartervile, the merchant, as a diabolic figure. In fact, whatever is consistent in Dekker's attitudes on social and economic problems is grounded in his usual acceptance of the traditional medieval principle, "the ethical significance of the economic action of the individual, whether subject or prince."[11] Friendly critics have described his mind as undoctrinaire or as conservative.[12] Although unoriginal, Dekker's view was radical enough, in the sense that he urged all the implications of the Sermon on the Mount as law for each man's conscience.

The comments made on *A Knight's Conjuring* and on *Work for Armorers* in a previous chapter have implied Dekker's fundamental atttitude toward the evil of poverty. *Work for Armorers* particularly challenges our attention, for it appears to deal as systematically with economics as anything he ever wrote. But to today's reader it may be quite unsatisfactory for the two reasons suggested in the preceding paragraph: Dekker traces the sources of economic hardship and oppression to individual self-ishness and greed, and he appears to identify wealth with money. True, in one place he does observe that the earth is liberal with her fruits, "powring forth her blessing to all thankfull creatures." Dekker also notes that poverty afflicts both the good and the bad, or at least the merely unfortunate as well as the vicious; for in Poverty's army he musters younger brothers, old soldiers, scholars, and serving men, along with bankrupts, panders, and the like.[13] But we must reject the inference that Dekker thought of wealth as resources operated on by labor or of the poor as victims of institutional or class-oppression. He does not think in these terms.

For Dekker, the liberality of nature shames mankind by its contrast to our avarice; and the poverty of a younger son or an old soldier is not something inevitable in the Elizabethan social system but the result of the immoral abuse of a divinely established order: the abuse arising from selfishness and avarice in fathers, elder brothers, and the king's ministers. The younger son and the old soldier, if they are thrifty and industrious in character, are poor only because the greedy who have money deny them their due. The chief and ultimate source of strangeness in Dekker's ideas on poverty is, I repeat, his identification of wealth with money. Of course he saw (no one better) that money buys goods and that goods may be hoarded as well as consumed. Yet Dekker regarded money as "the mother of *Plenty*," although she is almost universally locked up by her "councillors" against her "nature and condition."[14] He believes, with a rather painful simplicity, that the worst offenders against the poor are those who hoard money. Hoarding of grain, rack-renting, monopolizing and exporting of necessities are mere causes, in Dekker's view, of the primary evil of sequestering money from circulation.[15] Against usury he repeats the medieval argument: "The Vsurer liues by the lechery of mony, and is Bawd to his owne bags, taking a fee that they may ingender."[16]

If Jonson could perceive another source of economic injustice, an "almost Utilitarian individualism" growing out of Calvinism,[17] Dekker apparently could not see so deeply into the changes in his society. I find no speculations of that sort in his tracts; and his animus against Puritans seems to be caused by their threat to the Established Church and, of course, to the theater. The Bellman of London, in his serious classification of rascals, nowhere speaks of society's responsibility for their vice; the offenders are all sinners destined for Tyburn unless they repent. Dekker personifies the causes of Poverty, which he includes among her "councillors," as Discontent, Sloth, Carelessness, and Repining; but no public cause like Injustice is even mentioned.[18]

And yet, although Dekker is no social philosopher, his position is a respectable one. Like millions of his intelligent contemporaries, he takes the traditional view that the social evils of his world will find no cure except through reform of the consciences of the members of society. Ordinances, laws, "social action," are ineffective; for man's Babylonian heart is as fertile in evil as in good, and to repress greed or lust in one form or practice will only cause it to reappear in another. In a sense, Dekker is conservative; for although he sees that "all our courses are but figures of eight; the end of one giddie circle is but falling into a worse..." and that this is the "last and worst age of the world,"[19] yet, with neither cynicism nor despair he accepts the Elizabethan social order as the best yet given. To strive for radical change in it would be so futile that he does not even mention the idea. All men are faulty; hence the king, and even the lord mayor, must act as moderators "betweene the griping Rich and the wrangling Poore."[20]

Logically, having assigned ultimate responsibility for social betterment to the individual's conscience before God, Dekker interprets evil in terms of the cardinal sins. In our chapter on the tracts we have noted those that he harps on most—greed in its many forms, cruelty, pride, lust, and waste. As the offenses of the rich and powerful are the familiar ones, we should emphasize the sins with which Dekker charges the poor: thriftlessness, idleness or sloth, carelessness or indifference, waste, envy or hate of the rich[21]—not to speak of drunkenness, lust, and cruelty which they share with their betters. Dekker does not suppose that Newgate Prison, the Counters, or Bridewell will ever cease to be needed; they deter men from evil-doing and remove the vicious from society or rehabilitate them. On the other hand and quite characteristically, he condemns the cruelty of the rich who flee the city during the plague and make no provision for poor starving prisoners who lack the usual charity. In his view, relief of the poor by the rich is not simply a means for the rich to advance in love of God as a private virtue; rather, it is an obligation in conscience to sustain the less fortunate; "you be but Gods Almoners."[22] As Thomas Aquinas said, Christians owe each other more than simple justice, for the uncontrollable misfortunes of life also make mercy an obligation.

Dekker observes, of course, that social groups have their special habits of evil-doing. Courtiers are prone to prodigal waste, soldiers to murder, farmers to engrossment, tradesmen to rivalry and contention, scholars to heresy, and citizens to "city-sins"— forms of extortion, no doubt. But Dekker does not find in these propensities the signs of what we call "class warfare" or the indications of any class's major responsibility for social corruption. The conditions of their station provide each group with special temptations and lead, therefore, to characteristic sins. Dekker, perhaps because of his literary training, sometimes tends to take a sentimental view of country life as more moral than the "vndoing Cittie"; but he readily discards this foolishness.[23] He concludes that human nature is as prone to vice in one locality as in another. We may epitomize this account of his notions of social evil by citing Dekker's *Inferno* (Act V, Scene 2, of *If This Be Not a Good Play*) in which the five heinous sinners exhibited in the flames are two traitors, a prodigal, an extortioner, and a heretic.

Almost all Elizabethan writers at some time pause to lament the disintegration of the classes of society, an alarming symptom of disorder in the world. The hateful acquisitiveness that Jonson and Middleton present in their satiric drama is often especially associated with a desire to rise above one's station, an aspiration that must be condemned if it leads, as it always does in the Elizabethan view, to vice of some kind, or if it results from pride or avarice. Dekker probably accepted this objection to change of station in theory[24]; but in practice he seems more tolerant than other dramatists of the fact of increasing social mobility.

In fact, the characters in Dekker's plays cross class-boundaries very easily. Allowing for the heightening of both language and situation in romantic drama, we come nevertheless to respect the motives of an important citizen, Sir Roger Otley, whose character (not to speak of his wealth) is on a par with the Earl of Lincoln's. Sir Roger no more wishes his daughter Rose to marry the prodigal nephew of the Earl than does the Earl himself. The Lord Mayor decidedly prefers a conventional match, Rose's marriage to Hammon: "A proper gentleman,/A citizen by birth, fairly allide . . . /this gentleman" (I.1.44; II.2.57–62). But, as the king says, "Loue respects no bloud" (V.5.103); and Rose is "wel borne" (besides fair and virtuous) and "a worthy bride for any gentleman" (for *even* a gentleman). Sir Roger has to accept a marriage that certainly is advantageous for his daughter. Because Lacy has been technically a traitor for her sake, the king knights him and thus restores his honor and the Earl's (V.5.106, 111-113).

The loser, Hammon, comes close to seeming a ridiculous weakling. But Dekker probably intended no satire of the bourgeoisie. The citizen-gentleman, presumably a rich merchant's son, only vaguely represents a class. He shows himself honorable in his final gesture of generosity to Jane and Ralph. More significant than this is his willingness to take Jane, a tradesman's servant, for his bride.

If we may judge by this and the other plays and the tracts, Dekker does not view the fluidity of Tudor society with indignation or even disapproval. When he collaborates with Middleton on a "citizen comedy" like *The Roaring Girl,* he dulls the satiric point of his partner's ironic scenes both by continuing them in episodes of farce and by sentimental endings. When Dekker writes bourgeois comedy with John Webster, as in *Northward Ho!,* the farcical intrigue dominates throughout. In short, Dekker had little inclination for satire of the social classes or for comedy of manners. Certainly the characters of Matheo in Part II of *The Honest Whore* and of Horace in *Satiromastix* prove that Dekker lacked neither keen observation nor wit for the purposes of satire. But he was more interested in individuals than in types or classes. And this disposition is quite consistent with his moral outlook on life.

CHAPTER 6

Conclusion

IN briefly reviewing the formative influences upon Dekker as literary man and in appraising his accomplishment as dramatist and writer of tracts, we should note that the scholar who has most recently surveyed Dekker's career, Mme. Jones-Davies, has entitled him "a painter of London life," which he is, beyond question. As preceding chapters have shown, however, Dekker's plays exemplify the genres of moral fantasy, romance, comedy, and tragicomedy without being confined to the milieu of London or to a transcription of urban manners. We have found in his tracts a wide range of fantasy, moralism, satire, and topical interest by no means limited to bourgeois concerns. In short, Dekker is probably as completely representative of the Elizabethan Englishman as any individual writer can be. To say this is also, no doubt, to say that Londoners were more Englishmen than they were Londoners. At any rate, it would be a serious misconception to evaluate Dekker's accomplishment (as, of course, Mme. Jones-Davies does *not*) only in terms of the shopkeeper scenes in *The Shoemaker's Holiday.*

I *Formative Influences*

If we attempt to summarize the leading cultural influences that formed Dekker's mind and art, we recall that, like Shakespeare and Ben Jonson, Dekker received no more than a good grammar-school education. From it, however, he imbibed an enjoyment of the Latin poets that endured throughout his life, a taste for good literature in general, and the traditional Renaissance idea of the dignity of poetry as art and of its high function to instruct as well as to delight. Despite the hardships of his life, Dekker tried as a writer to remain true to that ideal, even when necessity forced him, late in life, to adopt the more frivolous purposes of Fletcherian drama. For example, his consistency explains the contrasting portraits of the sinful prodigal and the morally generous man that he introduces, rather forcibly, into an inferior comedy written with John Day, *The Wonder of a Kingdom* (*circa* 1623). However, as a student of Latin literature, Dekker is not comparable to Jonson; and the Classical influence on him, notably that of Plautine comedy, is far less discernible in his plays than in those of Jonson and Thomas Heywood.

The English Church was apparently his chief tutor in the Christian creed and in love of the Bible. A fundamental seriousness and tenderness in his nature responded to religion, and hence he gave to religion a lifelong reverence and loyalty. Neither his plays nor his tracts give any evidence of a mind troubled about doctrinal points, about Catholicism's claim to authority, or about the inroads of scientific and philosophical skepticism on dogma. If we may assume that Shakespeare's *King Lear* indicates a spiritual anguish suffered by its author, Dekker's plays offer no counterpart. He makes no reference to Montaigne or any other skeptical writer, and it is much to be doubted that he read any of them. We may surmise that during most of his life he was too busy for philosophical or scientific reading and, aside from devotional books, had to restrict himself largely to works that might be converted into plays or tracts. His plague pamphlets show a merely ordinary knowledge of medical theory; he gives to empirics (experimental scientists) the commonplace, scornful term of "quacksalvers," but no real consideration of their principles. His references to astrology are not very frequent and show no strong interest or belief in it. Probably he was not attracted to science by temperament.

More surprisingly, history, a field of humanistic learning that became germinal in Shakespeare's and Jonson's plays, does not seem to have seriously concerned Dekker. We have only the titles of half a dozen early plays to indicate that he, with collaborators, used British history and legend, and there are a few other titles pertaining to recent French history; with each of these it may be that Dekker's collaborator provided the play's outline. Dekker probably read English history in John Stow's and Raphael Holinshed's *Chronicles*, and read it rapidly to obtain only the substance for a projected play. But we have no evidence that his imagination was captivated by persons like Hotspur or Perkin Warbeck. Historical references in Dekker's tracts are sparse. Whether British or Classical, history appealed less to Dekker than did mythology, morality, and romance, which fed his imagination. We may infer that, like Shakespeare and Jonson, Dekker continued to read, but that he did so more desultorily and less purposefully than they.

Apart from religion, formal learning, and the impct of national and international events, such as the defeat of the Spanish Armada when Dekker was about sixteen, the major cultural force in his life was the theater. As a youth in London, he developed an intense gusto for the vital dramatic art prevailing there and an exhaustive knowledge of its conventions, as we have noted at the beginning of Chapter 2. Hence, he was instructed, professionally, in the same school as Shakespeare and Jonson, although Shakespeare came to it later in life than the two Londoners. The differences among the ultimate accomplishments of the three writers stem, of course, from the innate differences in genius and temperament; but we may note, in passing, that Dekker's inferiority is not due to a merely commercial view of the theater. As suggested above, he loved and therefore respected all literary art, including the drama, with lifelong devotion. His prologues and other critical remarks make this attitude unmistakable.

No doubt Dekker's clearest statement of his conception of dramatic art is the Prologue to *If This Be Not a Good Play* (1611). The Prince's Men at the Fortune theater had rejected the play; the Queen's Majesty's Servants at the Red Bull had produced it. We may lack a sufficiently clear notion of the difference in the repertories of the two theaters to appreciate fully the significance of these facts. However, the experience led Dekker to write a concise manifesto of the purposes of English drama as he thought these purposes should be and, no doubt, as such playwrights of the 1590's as Robert Greene and George Peele had conceived of them. After he has denounced the number of pretenders to poetic genius (he calls them *Changelings,* line 5) who clog the theaters and after he has criticized the rude workmanship and filthiness of their plays, he then observes that the (public) theaters are losing their audiences. He wishes for a true poet to appear, one who

> Can call the *Banished* Auditor home, And tye
> His Eare (with golden chaines) to his Melody:
> Can draw with *Adamantine Pen,* (euen creatures
> Forg'de out of th'*Hammer,*) on tiptoe, to *Reach*-vp,
> And (from *Rare silence*) clap their *Brawny hands,*
> T'*Applaud,* what their *charmd* soule scarce vnderstands.
> That Man giue mee; whose Brest fill'd by the *Muses,*
> With Raptures, Into a second, them infuses:
> Can giue an Actor, Sorrow, Rage, Ioy, Passion,
> Whilst hee againe (by selfe-same Agitation)
> Commands the Hearers.... (31–41)

This whole passage, insofar as its main concern is to describe the effect of poetry, rests squarely on the assumption that un-learned people, even those of limited intelligence ("Forg'de out of th'*Hammer*"), will be captivated by poetic art ("*charmd* soule")—specifically by the rhythm and sound of language ("his Melody")—and will eagerly seek to comprehend sentiments, no-tions, and ideas which they "scarce vnderstand." It follows, therefore, that a dramatist should be a man who has been born with genius and has been trained in poetry, who then experi-ences poetic truth with fervor ("Raptures") and conveys the ex-perience ("selfe-same Agitation") to actors and, through them, to the audience.

Dekker's high, perhaps Platonic, view of the sensitivity of laborers and tradesmen to poetic beauty in drama is most un-usual and therefore very striking as a formulation. No doubt, however, it is the only postulate on which Shakespeare and his fellows could have relied in writing their drama. We must ad-mire Dekker for abandoning the usual clichés about the rabble-ment. Not only is his statement honest and humane, but it also reminds us that most Elizabethan dramatists, although many of them were hacks, possessed an ideal of their occupation which prevented their becoming mere purveyors to the sensations of the mass audience (as, in general, Hollywood has been). Dekker's Prologue also strongly implies the Renaissance's belief in the function of the poet as teacher, for Dekker absolutely identifies

[*146*]

dramatic poets with *"True Sonnes"* of Phoebus (9): "And to bee such-a-*One*,/Our *Poet* (this day) striues, or to bee *None*:/Lend not (*Him*) hands for *Pittie*, but for *Merit*. . . . " (43–45).

To return to the matter of Dekker's early development, he probably achieved a practical mastery of dramaturgy sooner than his two greater competitors, Shakespeare and Jonson. When we are pressed to explain in terms more specific than those of "genius and temperament" why he has not left a legacy of drama comparable, say, to Jonson's, we may note, as one possible reason, that Dekker eschewed experiment, in contrast to Jonson's incessant, almost restless development. It can scarcely be doubted that Dekker found the dramatic traditions of legend, chronicle, interlude, and romance satisfying to his spirit and imagination; they had delighted him in his youth, and in maturity he believed he saw in them a scope for the moralizing purpose combined with pleasure that was the function of art as he understood it. Therefore, he continued to utilize older themes and conventions as long as possible. This is not simply to say that he was conservative by temperament. As the Elizabethan drama waned in the Stuart era, there was a restriction of the vision and the significance of the art that was not due solely to sparser talent among the poets. Like others, Dekker was conscious of the losses English drama was undergoing. But he lacked the wish, the time, and the learning to grapple with the artistic problem and perhaps to revitalize the old tradition. Jonson's attempt to challenge a changing society and culture with his innovations in form and method reveals his superiority to Dekker in intellect and thought, that is, genius.

Dekker's economic distress will always come to mind as a reason for his limited artistic achievement; but to mention it is only another way of saying that a man of genial, but not robust, personality, an imaginative writer lacking hard, practical sense, inevitably suffered from want of time (which Jonson had, because he achieved patronage) to meditate on his art and to correct his works fully. In short, Dekker's temperament, in one respect an element of his artistic strength, was in another way his enemy.

However careless he may have been about money, he was not so about art. No judgment about him has been more foolishly untrue than A. C. Swinburne's description of him as "shiftless and careless . . . reckless and sluttish," even "lazy"![1] The alleged deficiencies in Dekker's plays that have been charged to his maladroitness, his haste under pressure of need, or his carelessness have been to some degree reinterpreted and justified in preceding chapters. In sum, the critics have not always well understood the dramatist's intention because they have not understood and responded to his use of antique conventions. Of course, no student of Dekker will grant that all his apparent faults are really defects in our knowledge. In some places the dramatist dwells too long on a topic or sentiment, draws out a comic scene to the point of tedium, or relies too strongly on a stereotyped character. However, we do well to remember that, since he had to please his audience in order to live, we are objecting in some measure to Elizabethan taste, not just to Dekker's slovenly workmanship. In any case, Dekker is useful to the student of drama because in the conservatism of his technique he has left us a more inclusive catalogue of Elizabethan themes and conventions than any other writer except Thomas Heywood.

II *Dekker's Achievement in Drama*

In considering the absolute artistic merits of his plays, even the confident Swinburne hesitated to make an evaluation: "To do justice upon the faults of this poet is easy for any sciolist; to do justice to his merits is less easy for the most competent scholar and the most appreciative critic."[2] Any critic who has carefully studied Dekker, the dramatist, may well share Swinburne's humility. However, despite our still incomplete knowledge of Elizabethan dramatic tradition—for instance, of the conventions of symbolic action on stage—and despite the difficulties created by many collaborations in the Dekker canon, a concluding chapter requires some critical generalizations. We may introduce them by considering the matter of Dekker's technical faults, some of which, it will be seen, are misapplications of his actual skill.

We may begin with the commonplace charge of Dekker's weakness in structuring his play. But the critics have rarely taken the trouble to define the term *structure* or even to analyze the structural faults of his plays, although *Old Fortunatus* is apparently the one most often in mind. No doubt there is an ambiguity in the term: On the lower level, it denotes the degree of success achieved by the dramatist in choosing absorbing episodes for enactment and in relating these by means of motivation, narration, foreshadowing, and so on, in order to achieve maximum effects of clarity, suspense, and irony. In brief, on this level structure is the achievement of good theater.

On a higher level, on which a play, considered as a work of art, is expected to possess a theme and to communicate a significance of life, structure denotes the choice of episodes and their management, not merely for maximum dramatic effect, but for meaning; and theme now partly dictates the choice of episodes and the means used to relate them. As but one instance of a special means: In Part II of *The Honest Whore,* Bellafront and Hippolito halt the action for one hundred and thirty lines (IV.1.256–394) while they debate the rewards of a life devoted to lust. The subject is related to the theme of the play, and the debate is a structural element, whether for good effect or bad. Not only in this, but in other plays, Dekker certainly expected to be, and therefore should be judged as an artist, a dramatist who wished to communicate a meaning. However, criticism has strongly tended to view him either as naïve and childlike or as a thoughtless hack.

As was suggested above, the objection to his "carelessness of form" has often been made because of misunderstanding. For example, unless one perceives in *Old Fortunatus* a unifying theme in both the episodes of Fortune, Vice, and Virtue and the careers of Fortunatus and his sons, the so-called "masque" of the goddess seems to be mere spectacle grafted on to the legend. Hence, the "reckless" lack of unity among the elements of the play seems to negate the possibility of structure in terms of theme and to give even the plot itself the effect of "riotous inconsequence."[3] Perhaps the ultimate critical judgment on *Old Fortunatus* will be that Dekker's effort to weave the elements of his play into significant unity has not been successful. But to regret, as two recent critics have done, the loss of so much of "the pleasant old story" of Fortunatus, sacrificed aimlessly for the masque of Fortune, Vice, and Virtue, is painfully mistaken criticism.[4] In itself, the pleasant old story is puerile; and the Fortune episodes of the play are not really a masque.

It seems true to say that Dekker is not a master whose control of form in drama is a delight. Among his independent plays perhaps only in *The Shoemaker's Holiday* does he bring the elements of the work into almost perfect harmony and proportion. On the other hand, it is almost impossible to find in any of his plays an instance of a development of plot that is not prepared for or a loose end left in the dénouement. This fact suggests craftsmanship, not carelessness; Professor Harbage has well emphasized Dekker's mastery of technique.[5] Yet, having denied the general charge of Dekker's slovenly workmanship we may reasonably accuse him (like other dramatists) of sometimes violating proportion by expanding an episode or a speech unduly, to take advantage of theatrical appeal (as in the Bedlam scene in Part I of *The Honest Whore,* V.2.177–299) or to satisfy his own fondness for a theme (for example, the neglect of soldiers, in *If This Be Not a Good Play,* I.2.122–127). Such interruptions of progress or of tone are not usually sharp enough to constitute serious defects. In his management of subordinate plots, Dekker's ability to achieve coherence and relevance seems to be about equal to that of most other Elizabethans of the second rank, for instance, George Chapman and John Ford.

More valid than criticism of Dekker's careless structure is the charge that he sometimes fails in characterization, especially that he uses stereotypes frequently. A fairly long list of his type-characters has been given at the beginning of Chapter 2. Characterization is, of course, rarely to be described in absolute categories, as rounded or flat; it is ordinarily distinguished by degrees of difference within types. So considered, Dekker's ranges are wide. A rather familiar type is the benevolent father. At one end of Dekker's range is Sir Quintilian Shorthose (in *Satiromastix*), an automaton; at the other end is Orlando Friscobaldo (Part II of *The Honest Whore*), an unforgettable man. In between them fall Janicola (in *Patient Grissil*), Old Carter (*The Witch of Edmonton*), and others.

Because Dekker writes comedy, fantasy, romance, and tragicomedy, and borrows from morality and saint's legend—genres in which fullness of characterization is less important than in tragedy—his use of type-persons is less objectionable; occasionally it is more appropriate. Among dramatists with whom Dekker is comparable in other respects, for example, Chapman and Thomas Heywood, he is not inferior in his power of characterization. Since we have learned to relate character-drawing to other aspects of dramatic art more judiciously than did nineteenth-century critics, Dekker gains by the new perspective. But we have to grant that he often relied very heavily on the skill of the actor, for whom he provided no more than a familiar outline to be filled in.

Although a man whose business is giving pleasure to an audience at a play has a choice among several kinds of delight to offer, creating laughter inevitably becomes a primary concern for him. The Elizabethan tradition demanded comedy in all genres, and Dekker tried to comply with the demand. As was noted in Chapter 2, Dekker shows a strong perception of absurdity in human beings, combined, as everyone recognizes, with a warm pity for human suffering. By George Meredith's definition, the combination of ridicule with tenderness constitutes humor; but humorists differ according to the dominance of one component or the other. Fundamentally, Dekker is a more serious writer than he has usually been considered to be by those who have not believed his assertions in his prologues. His earnestness and his sympathy reduce his capacity to portray affectation, vanity, and self-delusion. Comic irony, either in action or in utterance, is rare in his plays; for his temperament did not favor the detachment requisite for irony.

Dekker uses clowns and other comic conventions noted in Chapter 2, as well as comic devices. Of all human traits the one that seems to have most amused Dekker is the unsuppressed volubility for which some readers may chiefly remember Simon Eyre and Sybil in *The Shoemaker's Holiday.* This ebullience is also characteristic of a number of Dekker's clowns, including Shadow, Babulo, Lapland, and Bilbo; and it is displayed by some persons who have a serious function: Bellafront (especially in Part I of *The Honest Whore*); Orlando Friscobaldo, Hircius and Spungius in *The Virgin Martyr;* Fideli in *The Whore of Babylon.* Unsupported by an actor's skill in grimace, gesture, and intonation, this volubility is somewhat tiresome to modern readers except in a few instances like Eyre's part when a flavor of irony in the character or the situation makes it more acceptable. Nevertheless, the loquacity somewhat increases the traditional humor of the clown's repertory, his absurd soliloquies, paradoxes, and prophecies—the same kinds of jokes that Shakespeare gives to Lancelot Gobbo, Costard, and Touchstone.

Dekker's other staple form of humor is absurdity in diction and puns. As we have seen, he regularly introduces a foreigner who speaks a comic dialect—Welsh, Irish, French, or Dutch. English speakers like Simon Eyre and Captain Tucca use far-fetched epithets, allusions, and comparisons. In Horace's apartment, Tucca greets the poets thus: "Why you bastards of nine whoores, the Muses, why doe you walk heere in this gorgeous gallery of gallant inuentions, with that whooreson poore lyme and hayre-rascall?" (*Satiromastix*, I.2.279–81). Such absurd use of allusions Dekker may have learned partly from Thomas Nashe's tracts; and he occasionally uses it, especially in his own tracts, in Nashe's manner to create an amusing incongruity between colloquial expression and a solemn idea. In *News from Hell* (II, 94) Satan is described as Paymaster of Perdition, Monsieur Malefico and Headwarden of the Horners. Conversely, low things are exalted; a cobbler's callat is called a Helen and her paramour Sir Paris in *The Wonderful Year* (134–135). The speech of many of Dekker's characters is almost a tissue of proverbs, tumbled out in ridiculous association.

Finally, Dekker may be compared with Shakespeare in his addiction to puns, although not in the success with which he uses them. For Dekker no chance is too trivial to be passed by; a devil is called a "*Helvetian*"; a tinker "honors God *Pan*." Sometimes, however, the puns may rise to the level of epigram, as when the clown in *Old Fortunatus* speaks of himself: "Apparell is but the shaddow of a man, but *Shaddow* is the substance of his apparell" (V.2.44–45).

With respect to his use of bawdy, Dekker is as liberal as most Elizabethan dramatists, including Shakespeare. In the matter of fondness for indecency it is hard to differentiate among the playwrights, but Dekker is by no means the worst. Following the conventions of the Elizabethan stage, he assigns the bawdy to almost any comic character, but especially to gallants, male and female servants, and citizens' wives; the relatively few witty young gentlewomen in his plays do not use it, as they often do in Shakespeare.

On the whole, we must grant that Dekker is not a highly successful comedian. Witty, vivacious dialogue is scarce in his plays. Although he was certainly aware of the value of dramatic irony, he does not create ironic situations with ease or exploit them well after he has created them. To illustrate his rudimentary handling of irony, we may compare the dialogue between Orlando Friscobaldo and his villainous son-in-law (whom Orlando serves in disguise in Part II of *The Honest Whore*) with the asides and soliloquies of disguised Justice Overdo in *Bartholomew Fair*. Jonson exposes the fatuity of the deceiver's mind and of his plans by means of a full verbal revelation of his successive frustrations and surprises; but Dekker is satisfied to present a few asides expressive of Orlando's disgust. Nor does Dekker attempt to draw satiric caricatures like Jonson's Zeal-of-the-Land Busy and Sir Epicure Mammon or like Middleton's Quomodo and Dampit, figures of vices dangerous to Jacobean society. His satires of vice and folly are sketchy and perfunctory.

In summary, we may say that Dekker's serious, sympathetic nature was attracted chiefly by the moralistic and romantic features of Tudor and early Elizabethan popular drama, but did not make much response to the sporadic examples of wit, irony, and caricature that occur in it. He had at hand, of course, a superb model for wit and irony in the comedies of John Lyly. To be quite exact, Dekker could have read Lyly's plays; but, because of his youth, it is unlikely that he attended them when they were performed at Paul's or the Blackfriars theaters. But in any case a remarkably small degree of Lyly's influence is discernible in Dekker's drama. Shakespeare's great debt to Lyly offers an instructive contrast.

In regard to the absolute merits of Dekker's drama, his plays are stronger than those of many of his competitors in three ways: their variety of theatrical effect; their literary style, including reproduction of actual speech and poetic eloquence; and their moralism. Since some of these characteristics have been touched on in preceding paragraphs, they will be mentioned only briefly here.

As we have noted, Dekker developed high technical skill in play-making, a fact acknowledged by modern scholars.[6] Although comparatively few scenes have extraordinarily powerful impact, and although we may feel, more doubtfully, that the resolution is weaker and less climactic than in a Middleton play, for instance, yet Dekker's drama has tempo; scene follows scene with a fascinating alternation of tenderness, broad humor, pathos, and suspense—in other words, with well-sustained excitement. If we limit our view to his unaided plays (although his collaborations tend to the same conclusion), we find that in at least three of seven plays—*Old Fortunatus, The Shoemaker's Holiday,* and Part II of *The Honest Whore*—Dekker emphasizes a theme by genuine artistry in handling structural elements such as parallel characters and situations.[7]

Whether he is using prose or verse, the colloquial style in Dekker's plays is usually vivid. The dialogue entertains us with its tissue of proverbialism and its constant, homely allusion to matters of everyday living. While this is a quality common to almost all Renaissance English dramatists, of course, it is notably strong in Dekker. More than most writers, he relished the picturesqueness and raciness in the speech of common people and noted its indications of character. Although he falls below Jonson in the power of discriminating lower-class persons by their speech, he probably equals Shakespeare in this respect and rivals both of them in sheer abundance of proverbs and realistic allusions. An amusing specimen, which happens to be an ironic one, is Dame Margery Eyre's attempt to give an impression of humility while planning her costume as the new Sheriff of London's lady: "How shall I looke in a hoode I wonder? perdie odly I thinke.... Indeede all flesh is grasse, and *Roger,* canst thou tel where I may buye a good haire?" (*The Shoemaker's Holiday,* III.2.33–38). Because of the liveliness of the dialogue, readers are able to tolerate the repetition of phrases which Dekker uses for humorous characterization and which would be less annoying in the theater.

As a writer of dramatic verse, Dekker usually pleases us with an iambic meter of energetic but varied rhythm in which fairly uniform masculine endings are softened by frequent run-on lines. He is distinctive in his fondness for rhyme; his sententious and emotional passages are likely to run through a succession of couplets. Whether he writes in blank verse or rhyme, he normally charms by melodiousness. His ear for vowel music and consonant patterns is as sensitive as his feeling for rhythm, with the result that, technically, Dekker's verse at its best is delightful. But because he often had to write to meet a deadline, Dekker sometimes lapses into roughness in the verse, even into something painfully close to doggerel.

With regard to figures of speech and imagery, Dekker occasionally achieves poignant, memorable lines; but in the main his expression moves at a level where it may be said to avoid triteness and platitude by its combination of homely allusion or strong sense-impression with melodiousness of sound. In the following passage, which is typical of his graceful lyricism in description, we note the effective pungency of such words as *sweating, franticke,* and *burning*:

> Oh pardon me: for to this place I come,
> Lead by my fate, not folly; in this wood
> With wearie sorrow haue I wandered,
> And three times seene the sweating Sun take rest,
> And three times franticke *Cynthia* naked ride,
> About the rustie high-waies of the skies
> Stucke full of burning Starres, which lent her light
> To court her Negro paramour grim night. (*Old Fortunatus,*
>   I.1.151—158)

Dekker's imagery is not drawn with highly significant frequency from any special aspects of life with the exception of numerous references to the sea and navigation. His Classical allusions are familiar ones in Renaissance poetry, though they are often given freshness by a touch of humor or homeliness.

When Charles Lamb asserted that Dekker "had poetry enough for anything," he was probably thinking, not only of passages of fancy such as the one just quoted, but also of more incisive, rhetorical lines, of which he gives an example, Orleans' description of the worldly wise people who sneer at love—"a swarme of fooles,/Crowding together to be counted wise" (*Old Fortunatus,* III.1.42–43). But Lamb's remark was too enthusiastic. The crises of violent passion in Dekker's plays are less successful than the descriptive passages. Dekker sometimes cannot distinguish bombast or sentimentality from poetic utterance of strong emotion. In *Satiromastix* Sir Walter Terrill fails to express anguish as he meditates, using these labored images, on the approaching night in which his bride will become the victom of King William Rufus:

> O Night, that Dyes the Firmament in blacke,
> And like a cloth of cloudes dost stretch thy limbes;
> Vpon the windy Tenters of the Ayre:
> O thou that hang'st vpon the backe of Day,
> Like a long mourning gowne: thou that art made
> Without an eye, because thou shouldst not see
> A Louers Reuels: nor participate
> The Bride-groomes heauen; o heauen, to me a hell:
> I haue a hell in heauen, a blessed cursse.... (V.1.1—9)

Finally, as to the moralism of Dekker's plays, he is, I have said earlier, a fundamentally serious writer. Therefore, one of the strangest blunders of a few early critics was to brand him a lewd writer and dismiss him from consideration, no doubt because of his bawdy jokes. In fact, more than most dramatists of his time, none of whom ever entirely forgets to make a moral judgment, Dekker clings to the morality-play tradition because it seems most apt for his purpose: to instruct in moral truth. As Professor Harbage expresses it, Dekker "wanted to make a living and to do people some good."[8] His confidence in the instructive power of art springs from an essential optimism about human life; in Mme. Jones-Davies's words, *"Il choisit la sagesse chrétienne."*[9] That philosophy includes a belief that, in spite of appearances, love and divine grace will prevail against the world's evil. Furthermore, the Renaissance theory of art assumed that humanity is capable of improvement and asserted that art has power to effect the change. Therefore, Dekker is optimistic, even buoyant. His spirit of hopefulness does not, of course, ensure achievement of artistry in his work. However, his attitude must be kept in mind as we study not only his best plays, but those written, during the weariness of age, according to the pattern of a new fashion which was inimical to the kind of moral outlook in which he had been bred.

III *Dekker's Non-Dramatic Work*

We may classify the topics of Dekker's tracts under the headings of their ostensible purposes. The plague pamphlets exhort his countrymen, especially Londoners, to renounce their vices and serve God justly and piously, for fear of the punishment of disease and death; but the sermon is made attractive by description of the horrors of the plague and by anecdotes, most of them humorously macabre. The satiric tracts, which are the ones most imitative of Thomas Nashe's technique, survey the rampant evils of London life in order to warn the innocent to avoid contact with the vicious, but more generally, and vaguely, to repel all men from the practice of vice. The literary attractions of this group of pamphlets are vivid fantasy and amusing tricks with language. A third kind constitutes exposés of rascality, which are modifications of earlier "cony-catching" pamphlets and which catalogue the commonest and most interesting of underworld disguises and cozenages in order to forewarn the public and to reduce crime. Dekker seems to have believed, perhaps truly, that these tracts were efficacious. A few works of more philosophic quality discuss the causes of poverty and war, but they lighten the seriousness of the topic by using fantasy as the genre.

Really the same in purpose as these, but different in genre, is *Penny-Wise, Pound-Foolish,* a moral tale of a prodigal young merchant who is reformed by his friend and by his long-suffering wife, a bourgeois Griselda. We may complete the list with two works intended for religious edification: *Dekker's Dream,* a poem in decasyllabic couplets, a vision of Judgment Day, Heaven, and Hell, which he intended as a solemn reminder of the brevity of life and the importance of preparing for the hereafter; and *Four Birds of Noah's Ark,* a manual of prayers in prose for many ages and classes of persons.

As in his plays, Dekker in his non-dramatic works grounds his thought on the premise that to overcome evil in human life is possible only through the reform of the individual's conscience and behavior by conformity to the Decalogue and the Sermon on the Mount. Similarly, if natural evils like epidemic and earthquake, which are manifestations of God's anger, are to be averted or limited, it will be on the same conditions: the purification of men's lives. In these assumptions, which were, of course, the common ones in his society, Dekker shows no originality. Also "medieval," that is, derived from Scholastic ethical doctrine, are most of his ideas on the problems of economics which he could not have conceived except as ethical questions. His appeal to his reading public, therefore, is actually an appeal to the individual's conscience; and he calls for the practice of justice, charity, industry, thrift, sobriety, and humility. He writes homilies, not analyses of social forces.

In Dekker's view, the cardinal sins are pride, avarice, and waste. They are cardinal because pride leads to oppression and cruelty toward the helpless; however, avarice and waste create suffering indirectly by creating poverty. The clue to Dekker's thinking in economic matters seems to be his conception of money as the essence of wealth. Thus, when a miser hoards money, he causes want; and when a wastrel pours money into luxury or dissipation, he destroys it, in effect, by giving it to parasites and other non-productive persons. Dekker's conception of money as wealth—the feeblest part of his social thought—is probably a vague reflection of Mercantilist theory, the prevailing economics of the sixteenth and seventeenth centuries. Perhaps also partly due to Mercantilism is Dekker's ambiguous attitude about war, which he justifies in a few passages. However, his constant lauding of the soldier's profession is not equivalent to a defense of war.

In neither secular nor religious beliefs was Dekker a Puritan. Dealing with social evils he constantly insists on the distribution of money as just pay for all labor according to its dignity and especially on the religious duty of charity toward the unfortunate and the oppressed. He does not revere the wealthy as if their accumulation were proof of virtuous industry and a reward of divine favor falling on saints elected to salvation. Although Dekker does not specifically attack this attitude, his position is clear. Furthermore, as a loyal member of the Church of England, he has no patience with those who would enforce on her a change in government or doctrine.

As a prose writer and the chief pamphleteer of the Jacobean age, Dekker stands above his rivals mainly for his style. Preceding writers of tracts had left no distinctive examples of artistic form but, instead, a profusion of satiric fantasy, invective, anecdote, reportage, and what not, which were sometimes mingled and sometimes separate, but, as a rule, crudely composed. Above all, Nashe's works, written in coruscating style, had aroused Dekker's admiration in youth. Although he derived little guidance about organization from Nashe's pamphlets, Dekker did make some advance in structuring his tracts, as we may see by comparing *The Wonderful Year* (1603) with *The Gull's Hornbook* (1608). However, Dekker's improvement in this respect is inconsistent, probably because his varied purposes and subjects constantly posed new problems of organization and because he had little time for planning and no good models as guide.

Dekker's progress in improving his style is somewhat steadier; and, in fact, he is superior to his rivals even in his first attempts. He does not begin his pamphleteering with obvious imitations of Nashe's bravura, but with a sober report and moral preachment, joining together subjects that have only an accidental association in time—James's accession and the plague. Later he tries Nashe's manner in satire on the vices of London; but by degrees this imitation disappears, and an easy, colloquial, pleasantly ironic tone becomes Dekker's best expression in prose. It is not always maintained, for his last plague pamphlets, written in his old age, return to a homiletic tone largely devoid of humor and vivacity. A reader wishing to sample the best of Dekker's tracts will do well to read *The Seven Deadly Sins of London* and *The Gull's Hornbook* for their vivacious style and satiric vignettes of London life, and *Work for Armorers* as a lively expression of a common point of view on the problem of poverty. Among the plague pamphlets the best is Dekker's first, *The Wonderful Year*.

A student of English literature obviously must acquaint himself with Dekker's tracts first, in order to understand his skill in popular prose style and his importance in transmitting it through the Stuart age; secondly, to learn the point of view of an intelligent Elizabethan toward his world; and, thirdly, to enjoy and profit from the pictures of life in city and country—information which, though casual, is "simply invaluable," according to a good opinion.[10] Dekker's only venture into the poetry of vision, *Dekker's Dream,* sometimes reaches eloquence but not sustained grandeur; it remains only a partially successful evocation of the world to come. But his view of this world, of his people and their city, wins us by a lively truth that makes it an indispensable part of Elizabethan literature. Compared to the greatest masterpieces of that great age, his art is flawed in several ways; yet many of his works will be enjoyed as long as there are speakers of the English tongue—a reward that, had he known of it, would have sweetened his poverty a little.

Notes and References

In these notes and in the Bibliography, the following works of scholarship are cited merely by the authors' last names: Gerald Eades Bentley, *The Jacobean and Caroline Stage*, III (Oxford, 1956); Fredson Bowers, *The Dramatic Works of Thomas Dekker*, I–IV (Cambridge, 1953–1961); E. K. Chambers, *The Elizabethan Stage*, III (Oxford, 1923); R. A. Foakes and R. T. Rickert, *Henslowe's Diary* (Cambridge, 1961); Mary L. Hunt, *Thomas Dekker* (New York, 1911); M. T. Jones-Davies, *Un peintre de la vie londonienne: Thomas Dekker* (Paris, 1958); and F. P. Wilson, *The Plague Pamphlets of Thomas Dekker* (Oxford, 1925).

Chronology

1. F. P. Wilson, "Three Notes on Thomas Dekker," *Modern Language Review*, XV (1920), 82–85; Mark Eccles, "Thomas Dekker: Burial Place," *Notes and Queries*, CLXXVII (1939), 157.

Chapter 1

1. For instance, we have his apostrophe in *A Rod for Runaways* (1625), p. 146, beginning, "O London! (thou Mother of my life, Nurse of my being)..." As for the year, the best indication is a statement in the Epistle to *English Villainies*

(1632) that he is now three score years old.

2. The passage is quoted by A. Dyce, editor, *The Works of Thomas Middleton* (London, 1840), I, xvi.

3. Not counting a multitude of short Latin phrases taken from both literary and other sources, I have noted in Dekker's independent plays and tracts about 149 longer quotations of Latin verse and prose, mainly verse. Among the authors identified by Dekker or that I have recognized, Virgil is most frequent, followed by Martial, Ovid, Horace, and Seneca in descending order.

I believe that Dekker also possessed some knowledge of Greek. In *Satiromastix, The Whore of Babylon,* and *The Double PP* he uses Greek names for several characters.

4. Dekker's Dutch is far closer to linguistic accuracy than his other conventional stage dialects. This is apparent to anyone who examines the dialects closely; and see David M. Greene, "The Welsh Characters in *Patient Grissil*," *Boston University Studies in English*, IV (1960), 171–180.

5. In the Epistle Dedicatory of *Wars, Wars, Wars* (1628) he writes to the Lord Mayor: "*Drums, Fifes, Ensignes, Pikes, and Shot doe now come Marching into your Parlors: I know not how to handle either;*

yet I handle all" (sig. A₃v). Again, "No Souldier [I], *yet my Pen playes the* Captayne..." (A₃v). Finally, in the Epistle to all Noble Soldiers, "If (noble Spirit) as well you may, you wonder/How I, who ne're fir'd Cannon, speake in Thunder..." (A₄v).

6. The many conjectures made by W. G. Fleay, nineteenth-century historian of Elizabethan drama, with regard to Dekker's later revisions of the plays he wrote for Henslowe, 1594–1598, are unprovable and therefore futile. For comment on the conjectures see Chambers, pp. 300–305; for a list of the plays, see the section "Some Conjectural Revisions" of the Bibliography.

In 1598 Francis Meres named Dekker among the fourteen leading poets of England eminent "for tragedy" (*Palladis Tamia*, sig. Oo₃r). Of Dekker's plays up to 1598 none has survived in its original form and certainly no tragedy in any form. Apparently, some of the lost plays were tragedies.

7. For a conjecture about one puzzling item, see W. L. Halstead, "Dekker's Arrest for Debt by the Chamberlain's Men," *Notes and Queries*, CLXXVI (1939), 41–42.

8. In *Cynthia's Revels* the Elizabethan audience may have been able to detect some hits at Dekker, but I cannot believe that Jonson intended any of the persons as a full caricature of Dekker. Jonson's essential purpose in the play was far other than to ridicule his enemies.

9. At the accession of King James, the Lord Admiral's Company became Prince Henry's Men until the Prince's death in 1612.

10. For instance, the picture of the damask-coated citizens who "so plye themselues with penny pots ... powring into their fat paunches, that at length they have not an eye to see withall...." (*The Seven Deadly Sins of London*, p. 42) or "...to drink vp the day and night in a *Tauerne*, loathsome" (*Work for Armorers*, p. 97).

11. The text of *Sir Thomas Wyatt* now extant is "a corrupt memorial reconstruction" (Bowers, I, 399); it probably is a debased version of one or both parts of *Lady Jane*, written for Henslowe in 1602 and revived by the Queen's Men about 1605. See the Bibliography, I.A, for 1602.

12. The satire against citizens in Part I of *The Honest Whore* and in *The Roaring Girl* is subordinate to romantic and moral themes and is largely the work of Middleton. Fleay is right in assigning *The Roaring Girl* to 1605.

13. For further discussion of the remuneration of the tract-writer, see Chapter 3.

14. As he tells at the end of *Dekker's Dream*, p. 60.

15. *The Witch of Edmonton*, with Ford and Rowley (1621); *The Bellman of Paris*, with Day (1623); *The Fairy Knight*, with Ford (1624); and *The Late Murder in Whitechapel*, with Ford, Rowley, and Webster (1624).

16. C. J. Sisson, *Lost Plays of Shakespeare's Age* (Cambridge, 1936), pp. 80–124.

17. To say that "Dekker sold" *Match Me in London* and *The Wonder of a Kingdom* is only an inference, but one based on three facts: (1) the printer's copy seems to have been in Dekker's autograph; (2) his name is correctly spelled on the title page; and (3) a Latin motto appears on the title page, according to his habit. A less likely alternative is that fair copies purchased from Dek-

ker some years before were now sold by the actors to the publishers.

In 1630 was also published Part II of *The Honest Whore,* which in 1608 had been entered in the Register to Thomas Man, but without payment of fee, and which was now re-entered without transfer from Man to Nathaniel Butter, the publisher. Dekker's name is correctly spelled on the title page, but there is no Latin motto. The printer's copy appears to have been Dekker's autograph. It is doubtful whether Dekker sold two different manuscripts of the play to Man and to Butter or whether the actors sold the "foul papers" of the play to Butter.

18. Eccles, "Thomas Dekker," p. 157.

Chapter 2

1. "The Prologue," *A Challenge for Beauty, The Dramatic Works of Thomas Heywood,* V (London, 1874, 4-5.

2. Although papal excommunication of Queen Elizabeth in 1570 marks the beginning of suppression of the medieval cycles and other religious drama, Phillip Stubbes, in *The Anatomie of Abuses,* 1583, speaks of mysteries as still being produced. The passage is quoted in Chambers, *Elizabethan Stage,* IV, 222.

3. C. H. Herford, *Studies in the Literary Relations of England and Germany in the Sixteenth Century* (Cambridge, 1886), pp. 210, 405–406. The earliest Dutch translation held by the British Museum is dated 1631. Its title page says it is *De achte mael herdruckt,* but whether the seven previous printings were in Dutch is uncertain. Probably more German versions than Dutch translations had been published by 1596. Miss Hunt suggests (p. 34) that Dek-

ker went to the Netherlands in his youth and there read a German version.

4. But the *Volksbuch* of 1509, apparently the first edition, was not divided into parts, and I have not seen any record of later publication in parts. The first known English translation was entered in the Stationers' Register as *The History of Fortunatus* on June 22, 1615. Edward Arber, *A Transcript of the Registers of the Stationers of London; 1554–1640* A.D., III (London, 1876), 568.

5. The "31 of November," says Henslowe.

6. Professor Fredson Bowers has found a cancellation in the quarto which suggests that possibly two thirds of the edition had been sold by mid-February, 1601. "Essex's Rebellion and Dekker's *Old Fortunatus,*" *Review of English Studies,* III (1952), 365–366.

7. At the end of 1597 Henslowe stops recording the names of plays when entering his share of the proceeds from productions. But he refers to plays by name in other connections, for instance, payments to dramatists and purchases of costumes and properties.

8. This is also Professor Bowers's opinion, I, 107. Henslowe's phrases are "for the altering of the book" and "for the end of *Fortunatus* for the Court." Foakes and Rickert, pp. 127, 128.

9. Herford, *Studies,* pp. 215–218.

10. Herford, *Studies,* p. 216.

11. She has to be told why Ampedo was punished (it was for sloth), lines 275–276.

12. Herford, *Studies,* pp. 217–218.

13. L. M. Manheim, "The King in *The Shoemaker's Holiday,*" *Notes and Queries,* CCII (1957), 432–433.

14. Alfred Harbage, "The Mystery of *Perkin Warbeck*," in *Studies in the English Renaissance Drama*, ed. by Josephine W. Bennett, Oscar Cargill, and Vernon Hall (New York, 1959), p. 137.

15. Although *The Weakest* was published in 1600, other evidence suggests, without proving, a considerably earlier date of composition than that of *Shoemaker's Holiday*. In *The Weakest* I cannot find any real evidence of Dekker's authorship; but Miss Hunt thinks he revised it (pp. 42–45).

16. It is well praised by Una M. Ellis-Fermor, *The Jacobean Drama* (London, 1947), p. 124.

17. E. W. Talbert, "The Purpose and Technique of Jonson's *Poetaster*," *Studies in Philology*, XLII (1945), 226, 251–252.

18. Dekker and Middleton's original title, judging by Henslowe's entry in his *Diary* before March 14, 1604, and by the entry in the Stationers' Register on November 9, 1604, was *The Humors of the Patient Man, the Longing Wife, and the Honest Whore*. Later Dekker decided to title the play *The Converted Courtesan*, which is the running title of the corrected edition. Meantime, however, the first edition had appeared as *The Honest Whore, with the Humors*, etc.; and, because of the popularity of Part I, this title was also used for Part II. On the appropriateness of *The Converted Courtesan* as the title, see Michael Manheim's excellent article, "The Thematic Structure of Dekker's *2 Honest Whore*," *Studies in English Literature 1500–1900*, V (1965), 363–81.

19. After studying the texts of a number of Middleton's plays, and having twice made an analysis of the bibliographical and stylistic evidence both in Part I of *The Honest Whore* and in *The Roaring Girl*, I find that to the former play Middleton contributed between seven and eight hundred lines. His undoubted scenes are I.5, III.1, and III.3. Of very doubtful authorship are IV.2 and IV.3. However, it is apparent that Middleton is chiefly responsible for the scenes of the testing of Candido. Although Professor Bowers does not make a conjecture on the matter, I believe that the printer's copy was entirely in Dekker's handwriting; but if this is true, the fact would not preclude the presence of traces of Middleton's spelling and punctuation in the manuscript.

20. Furthermore, Middleton's contribution (especially I.5 and III.1), which is indeed more realistic than the rest of the play, is not impressively so, for it consists of ironic farce and attributes to Candido's wife a motive for her shrewishness (resentment) which is simpler than the perversity which Dekker suggested in I..4.

21. In the verse of Part I this quadrisyllable several times appears as "Infaeliche," presumably an Anglicized spelling of the Italian pronunciation.

22. The long show of Bridewell birds which follows Matheo's confession, "And I am now his Patient," V.2.192, allows ample time for him to show his change of heart by caressing Bellafront, though he does not speak.

23. The title page bears his name correctly spelled and a Latin motto, *Vexat Censura Columbas*; he supplies a full apparatus of *Drammatis Personae*, epistle *Lectori*, and theater *Prologue*; and the text of the play was in his own handwriting. He

made some revisions for publication.

24. *Lectori,* line 39. See also Chapter 1.

25. The wording of the first clause in the title is that found in the head title and head lines of the quarto and is, therefore, probably Dekker's own. The title page has *If It Be Not Good,* etc., no doubt a printer's alteration.

26. Herford, *Studies,* p. 302.

27. The priory has been penetrated by avaricious Barterville in disguise as a friar and has been handed over by corrupted Alphonso to a courtier. It surely represents ecclesiastical institutions or the English Church in general. "Woe to these dayes,/When to raise Vpstarts, the poor CHVRCH decays," III.3.122–123.

28. See the dedication to the Queen's Men and the Prologue, which proudly asks the audience, "Lend not [the poet] hands for *Pittie,* but for *Merit,*" 45. In the Epilogue, "Much Labour, Art, and Wit, make vp a Play," 7.

29. Herford, *Studies,* p. 317.

30. The Prologue to *If This Be Not* is Dekker's finest expression of his aims as a dramatist. I have discussed its chief ideas in the first section of Chapter 6.

31. *Match Me in London* was licensed for production by Sir Henry Herbert on August 21, 1623, as an "old play" formerly allowed by Sir George Buc. But the quoted phrase is one Herbert used for any play formerly licensed, whether recently or not; and Buc was still licensing in 1622. The title page of the first edition (1631) says the play was first produced at the Red Bull Theatre and later at the Phoenix. Dekker wrote for the Queen's Men about 1611 and for the Revels Company in 1619–1622—both of them occu-

pants of the Red Bull. Professor G. E. Bentley favors the earlier date, *The Jacobean and Caroline Stage,* I (Oxford, 1941), 185, note 5. But Dekker's dedication to Carlell in 1631 says nothing of any revision, which one would expect for the Phoenix production of a play from 1611 (the Phoenix opened in 1617). Therefore, I believe that *Match Me* was originally played about 1620 by the Revels Company at the Red Bull and, after that company's extinction in 1622, by the Lady Elizabeth's at the Phoenix and by their successors, Queen Henrietta's Company. See Bentley, *Jacobean and Caroline Stage,* I, 165–169, 182–187, 219.

The difficulty in dating *Match Me* is typical of a number of Dekker's plays.

32. See IV.1.14–15; but the arrival of a party of ladies-in-waiting, II. 4.48, surely implies a royal command.

33. See III.3.44–47. The ambiguity is typical of tragicomedy.

34. Harbage, "Mystery of *Perkin Warbeck,*" pp. 130–131, 137.

35. A. C. Swinburne, "Thomas Dekker," *The Nineteenth Century,* XXI (1887), 102; M. C. Bradbrook, *The Growth and Structure of Elizabethan Comedy* (London, 1955), p. 121.

Chapter 3

1. Examples of satisfactory attempts to use scholarly technique in studies of attribution are collected in a volume of essays edited by Ephim G. Fogel and David V. Erdman, *Evidence for Authorship* (Ithaca, 1967).

2. Henslowe's *Diary* furnishes this and other information about the play's genesis and first production. There is evidence that *Grissil* was

successful; see Bowers, I, 209, and Harold Jenkins, *The Life and Work of Henry Chettle* (London, 1934), pp. 153–156.

3. Jenkins, *Chettle*, pp. 166–167.

4. *Ibid.*, p. 167.

5. David M. Greene, "The Welsh Characters in *Patient Grissil*," *Boston University Studies in English*, IV 1960), 171–180.

6. Jenkins, *Chettle*, pp. 168–169.

7. Bowers, I, 211.

8. Professor Bowers comments: "The manuscript serving as printer's copy seems to have been a collection of papers written in two different hands, in large part coinciding with conventional estimates of the division of authorship" (III, 367). Bowers does not even mention the possibility of Massinger's being the reviser of Dekker's old play—a theory that would be very hard to reconcile with the evidence of collaboration summarized in his "Textual Introduction."

9. In medieval lives of the martyrs "a strain of jests and comedy" to ridicule and frustrate pagan tormenters is characteristic of the genre. See Douglas Cole, "Hrotsvitha's Most Comic Play: *Dulcitius*," *Studies in Philology*, LVII (1960), 597–605.

10. The title page of the first edition, 1658, says: "By divers well-esteemed Poets; *William Rowley, Thomas Dekker, John Ford*, &c." The *et cetera* has generally been ignored by scholars, although the title page offers true details about the performances of the play which should lead one to consider possible significance in the &c.

11. Dewar M. Robb, "The Canon of William Rowley's Plays," *Modern Language Review*, XLV (1950), 139. See also H. Dugdale Sykes, "The Au-

thorship of *The Witch of Edmonton*," *Notes and Queries*, CLI (1926), 457; and Hunt, p. 181.

12. Bowers, III, 485.

13. As mentioned in Chapter 1, above, we know a good deal about one of the other three, *The Late Murder in Whitechapel, or, Keep the Widow Waking.*

14. This is also true of the court masque. Stephen Orgel says that the masque world is "one of ideal abstractions and eternal verities." *The Jonsonian Masque* (Cambridge, Mass., 1965), p. 73. Mrs. Dolora Cunningham believes that the masque incites the audience to "conscious moral imitation of the virtues" of true kingship. "The Jonsonian Masque as a Literary Form," *ELH*, XXII (1955), 109.

15. Ellis-Fermor, *Jacobean Drama*, p. 120; see also Harbage, "Mystery of *Perkin Warbeck*," p. 137.

Chapter 4

1. Nashe published at least two, Greene about seven, tracts in 1592.

2. A valuable sketch of the surge of tract-writing at this time is that written by C. S. Lewis, *English Literature in the Sixteenth Century Excluding Drama* (Oxford, 1954), pp. 394–418.

3. R. B. McKerrow, *An Introduction to Bibliography for Literary Students* (Oxford, 1948), p. 134.

4. I exclude from this total the new titles of tracts revised and reissued. *News from Hell* became *A Knight's Conjuring*; and *Lanthorn and Candlelight* became *O per se O*, then *Villainies Discovered*, then *English Villainies.*

5. *Lanthorn*, which is a sequel of *The Bellman of London* and an exposé of vice and swindling, enters the class of satire.

6. Nashe had used the traditional seven in *Pierce Penniless;* Dekker presumably wished to avoid repetition.

7. *Seven Deadly Sins,* p. 61.

8. Pierce is partly a conventional satyr, the mask of the satiric poet, not at all the ideal poet. See Alvin Kernan, *The Cankered Muse* (New Haven, 1959), p. 149.

9. An unpaid debt of Charon's amounts to one penny for the use of the cucking stool at Pyriphlegeton to punish a *"Cobler of Poetrie,* called a *Playepatcher,* [who] was condemned with his Catte to be duckt three times ... because he scolded against his betters, and those whom hee liued vppon, laid out at that time for straw, to haue carried pusse away if she had kittend, to auoyd anie catterwalling in Hell. . . . ," p. 146 (I quote from the quarto, sigs. I_3–I_3v). This I take to be a reference to Ben Jonson in some domestic trouble. See J. F. Bradley and J. Q. Adams, *The Jonson Allusion Book, 1597–1700* (New Haven, 1922), p. 54.

10. See Chapter 5 for discussion of this point.

11. John Awdeley, *The Fraternity of Vagabonds* (1565); Thomas Harman, *A Caveat to Common Cursitors* (1567); Robert Greene, *A Notable Discovery of Cozenage* (1591), and a number of sequels by Greene. Dekker's appropriations from these and other writers are described by E. H. Miller, "Thomas Dekker, Hack Writer," *Notes and Queries,* CC (1955), 145–150.

In Haughton's *Englishmen for My Money* (1598), one of the bellman's cries is given: "Maydes in your Smocks, looke wel to your Locks,/ Your Fier and your Light; and God giue you good night." Malone So-ciety edition (1912), lines 1669–1670.

12. The British Museum *Catalogue* quotes the title page of the "third impression," 1608, as claiming to possess "new aditions." If they really exist, Dekker was probably paid something for them.

13. F. B. Williams, *Index of Dedications and Commendatory Verses in English Books before 1641* (London, 1962), p. 49, identifies the "Io: Da:" who initials the first poem as *"supposedly* Davies of Hereford." But as a matter of probability (xxvii), Dekker's collaborator in playwriting seems much likelier.

14. Miller, "Thomas Dekker," p. 149.

15. The popularity of the "Canters Dictionarie" in Chapter I of *Lanthorn* led Dekker to add an episode to *The Roaring Girl* (V.1. 56–278) to exploit rogues' cant further. The play was originally composed about 1605. The actual roaring girl who gave her name to the heroine, Mary Frith, was induced by the Prince's Men to appear on the Fortune stage after one or more performances of the play. F. W. X. Fincham, "Notes from the Ecclesiastical Court Records at Somerset House," *Transactions of the Royal Historical Society,* 4th series, IV (1921), 112–113.

16. It was much revised by Samuel Vincent and issued as *The Young Gallant's Academy* in 1674.

17. Herford, *Studies,* p. 389. *Grobianus* was first published in Latin in 1549 at Frankfort and ran through many editions, first in Latin, then in German, in the sixteenth century; but I know of no recorded Dutch, French, or English translations before *The Gull's Hornbook.* See Gustav Milchsack, *Neudrucke deutscher Litteraturwerke,* Nos. 34–35 (Halle, 1882), xiv–xxxiii.

18. Herford, *Studies,* p. 391. The epistle "To the Reader" of *Hornbook* tells that Dekker had begun a versified translation of *Grobianus* "long since," but (perhaps in 1609) abandoned that task in favor of a tract.

19. Dekker seems to date its epistle April 15; see p. 177. The plague was more prevalent than usual in 1609, and the theaters were probably closed most of the calendar year. F. P. Wilson, *The Plague in Shakespeare's London* (Oxford, 1963), p. 125.

20. His only book of devotions, says F. P. Wilson, *Foure Birds of Noahs Arke* (New York, 1925), p. vi; but *Dekker's Dream* (1620) is a religious work in intention, though it is not devotional, strictly speaking.

21. *Foure Birds,* ed. by Wilson, pp. 284–285.

22. I understand another hit at Jonson in one passage: "*Item.* I giue my inuisible cloakes to all Bankrouts, because they made them, but to one Poet onely (called *Poet Comedy)* I giue my best inuisible Cloake, because it onely fits his shoulders better then mine owne; but chiefly for that hee will trim it vp wel, and line it with *Come not neere me,* or *stand further off;* And because he is a slip of mine owne grafting, I likewise bequeath to him my best Slippers, to walke and play with his Keepers noses" (p. 353, but quoted from the quarto, sig. E). Chronologically, perhaps, this jibe would fit more plausibly after the failure of *Sejanus* (1603), when Jonson was living with Daubigny, rather than in the late 1590's.

23. *Catchpolls' Masque,* p. 367.

24. Entered in the Stationers' Register on October 11, 1619, perhaps published in December. The title page has a quaint woodcut of the author asleep.

25. Curiously, there are passages of Senecan prose in the preliminaries of *A Strange Horse-Race,* as well as others in its first part.

26. *Dekker's Dream,* pp. 24–25. A briefer sketch of the general resurrection is given by Donne in the seventh of the "Holy Sonnets"; it is possible that Dekker had read the poem.

27. Including *Penny-Wise, Pound-Foolish,* entered in the Register as by Dekker.

28. Described more factually and impressively by William Thomas, *The History of Italy,* 1549, sigs. Y_4 verso-Z_1.

29. Sig. B_3 recto.

30. II.1.102–119.

31. See Kernan, *Cankered Muse,* Chapter 3.

32. See the Bibliography, "Authentic Works," for comments on Dekker's contributions to the Overbury and Mynshull books of characters in 1616 and 1617.

Chapter 5

1. *A Rod for Runaways,* p. 144.

2. *If This Be Not a Good Play,* IV.1.10–13; *The Seven Deadly Sins,* pp. 21, 44; Gregg, *Thomas Dekker: A Study in Economic and Social Backgrounds* (Seattle, 1924), pp. 95–96.

3. *Four Birds,* p. 162; *Seven Deadly Sins,* p. 7.

4. Wilson, *Plague in Shakespeare's London,* pp. 3–4.

5. *A Rod for Runaways,* p. 142.

6. *Wars, Wars, Wars* (1628), sig. B_2 verso; *A Rod for Runaways,* p. 146.

7. *The Dead Term,* p. 63.

8. Sigs. B_2 recto, B_8 verso; and *The Dead Term,* p. 64.

9. *News from Graves-End,* p. 86. See also *Jests to Make You Merry,* pp. 345–355; *Work for Armorers,* p. 91; and especially *If This Be Not a Good Play,* I.2.122–137, a classic indictment of Elizabethan neglect of veterans.

10. On the early Mercantilists see, for instance, L. H. Haney, *History of Economic Thought* (New York, 1949), Chapter VII, especially p. 112.

11. Edwin R. A. Seligman, "Economics: The History of Economic Thought," *Encyclopedia of the Social Sciences* (New York, 1937), III, 346. Perhaps, however, it is partly Mercantilist theory which causes Dekker to affirm "Learning! and Armes! and Traffique! the triple wall/That fortifies a Kingdome..." (*If This Be Not Good,* II.1.171–172).

12. Gregg, *Dekker,* p. 71; Patricia Thomson, "The Old Way and the New Way in Dekker and Massinger," *Modern Language Review,* LI (1956), 169.

13. *Armorers,* pp. 143, 116–123.

14. *Armorers,* pp. 144–145.

15. *Armorers,* pp. 145–149.

16. *Seven Deadly Sins,* p. 28.

17. See L. C. Knights, *Drama and Society in the Age of Jonson* (London, 1937). The quoted phrase is from R. H. Tawney, *Religion and the Rise of Capitalism* (Harmondsworth, 1938), p. 205.

18. *Armorers,* pp. 112–116.

19. *A Knight's Conjuring: Done in Earnest, discovered in Jest,* ed. E. F. Rimbault, Percy Society Publications, Vol. V (London, 1841), 15; *Bellman,* p. 66.

20. *Britannia's Honor,* lines 30-31.

21. *Armorers,* pp. 145–149.

22. *Rod for Runaways,* p. 149. Dekker's defense of Bridewell and other prisons is stated in Part II of *The Honest Whore,* V.2.21–53 (the Master's long exposition) and in *Seven Deadly Sins,* pp. 69–70.

23. *Lanthorn and Candlelight,* p. 208; *Armorers,* pp. 153–154; *Bellman,* pp. 70–72, 112–113.

24. See Janicola's counsel to his discontented son Laureo, *Patient Grissil,* IV.2.8-20; also V.2.214–218. However, Laureo's is the special case of a poor scholar ambitious to be a counsellor of his Prince.

Miss Thomson, in the article cited in note 12, differs from my interpretation. She thinks that in *Shoemaker's Holiday* Dekker depicts the old, feudal society, not the more fluid Tudor one. Dekker, she believes, does not exploit social tensions, even ignores realism in favor of romance. Pages 169–175. But her case is founded only on *Shoemaker's Holiday.*

Chapter 6

1. Swinburne, "Thomas Dekker," pp. 82, 87, 102.

2. *Ibid.,* p. 102.

3. Ellis-Fermor, *Jacobean Drama,* pp. 118, 121.

4. Thomas M. Parrott and Robert H. Ball, *A Short View of Elizabethan Drama* (New York, 1958), pp. 107, 113.

5. Harbage, "Mystery of *Perkin Warbeck,*" pp. 130–131, 137.

6. For instance, by Ellis-Fermor, *Jacobean Drama,* p. 120, as well as by Harbage (note 5, above).

7. See the discussion of these three plays in Chapter 2. Recent doctoral dissertations by Profs. James H. Conover and Leonard M. Manheim are devoted to structure in Dekker's plays.

8. Harbage, "Mystery of *Perkin Warbeck,*" p. 140.

9. Jones-Davies, p. 86.

10. A. H. Bullen, "Dekker, Thomas," *Dictionary of National Biography.*

Selected Bibliography

I. PRIMARY SOURCES

As noted at the beginning of the Chronology preceding Chapter 1, the large number and the attribution of Dekker's anonymous writings often call for at least brief explanation on many items and therefore justify placing the chronological list under "Primary Sources." Professor Fredson Bowers's definitive edition in four volumes, *The Dramatic Works of Thomas Dekker* (Cambridge: Cambridge University Press, 1953–1961), does not attempt to name the lost plays or even all the extant ones which good authority has attributed to Dekker; for instance, *Blurt, Master Constable* and *The Tell-Tale*. Likewise, F. P. Wilson's edition, *The Plague Pamphlets of Thomas Dekker* (Oxford: Oxford University Press, 1925), offers only part of the tracts. Alexander B. Grosart's *The Non-Dramatic Works of Thomas Dekker* in four volumes (London: Privately printed, 1884–1885) needs correction by exclusions and inclusions. For these reasons, the Dekker canon should be surveyed.

Any attempt to compose the canon raises three major problems in addition to the obvious difficulty with chronology. They are: (1) doubtful ascription of extant complete plays, tracts, and poems—or, more precisely, deciding the validity of the

evidence on which such ascription has been made; (2) the identity of certain lost plays and other works, in instances where references to them are obscure; and (3) Dekker's contribution to extant works, mainly plays, in which he is known to have collaborated with other writers. It soon becomes apparent that in these and other problems of canon a sound decision can result only from judicious sifting and weighing of the external and internal evidence—in other words, from the knowledge and good judgment of the investigator.

The following bibliography is offered with only the general statement that my examination of the Dekker canon began long ago and has continued intermittently in connection with related studies on Middleton. During the preparation of this book, I have analyzed Dekker's literary style and his habits of spelling and punctuation. And for those works about which real questions of authenticity arise, I have consulted most of the scholarship.

A chronological arrangement of Dekker's works is justified because any other order would obscure the time-relationship which is sometimes important in solving difficulties about authorship. Each work, then, is assigned to its presumed date of composition; but the date of the first edition is also given if it is later than the date of composition. When no date of publication is specified, it is the same as that of composition. Finding particular titles is easy through the index of this volume.

Under "Authentic Works," are listed those works for which there is genuine reason to suppose Dekker's responsibility by himself or with collaborators. The works listed under "Works Wrongly Ascribed to Dekker" are extant and are those for which Dekker's authorship has been proposed, but in which I personally think he had no share. The canon given by Mme. M. T. Jones-Davies in *Un peintre de la vie londonienne: Thomas Dekker*, II (Paris: Didier, 1958), 339–416, is different chiefly because of her inclusion of all works which have ever been attributed to Dekker. She distinguishes the attributions that are false and those that are doubtful; I have simply omitted those works that seem both false and unsupported by adequate scholarship.

In the annotations I refer to a number of often-cited works of scholarship only by their authors' last names; these works are listed at the beginning of "Notes and References." Citations of F. G. Fleay's *A Biographical Chronicle of the English Drama, 1559–1642*, a two-volume work (London: Reeves and Turner, 1891), are taken from Bentley and Chambers.

All primary sources listed here, if they were printed at all, were published in London.

A. AUTHENTIC WORKS

[1594?]. *The Jew of Venice* (lost play). In the Stationers' Register for 1655 entered as by "Tho: Decker." Possibly identical with either *The Venetian Comedy* or

The French Doctor, mentioned by Henslowe in 1594 without the authors' names.

[1595–1596?]. *The Play of Sir Thomas More*, apparently a collaboration with Anthony Munday, Henry Chettle, Thomas Heywood, and Shakespeare. First published in 1844. Bowers reprints the thirty-one lines of the manuscript that are in Dekker's handwriting, I, 3–5. See also *The Malone Society Collections*, VI (Oxford: Oxford University Press, 1962), 177–192.

1598. *Phaeton* (lost play). Henslowe paid for the book by "Mr. Dicker." In December, 1600, Henslowe paid Dekker for altering the play for a performance at court.

1598. *The Triplicity of Cuckolds* (lost play). Henslowe gives Dekker's name.

1598. *The Famous Wars of Henry I* (lost play), with Drayton and Chettle. Henslowe names the authors.

1598. *Godwin and His Three Sons* (lost play), with Drayton, Chettle, and Wilson, all named by Henslowe.

1598. *Pierce of Exton* (lost play), with Drayton, Chettle, and Wilson, all named by Henslowe.

1598. *Black Batman of the North* (lost play), with Drayton, Chettle, and Wilson, all named by Henslowe.

1598. Part II of *Godwin* (lost play), with Drayton, Chettle, and Wilson, all named by Henslowe.

1598. *The Madman's Morris* (lost play), with Drayton and Wilson, all named by Henslowe.

1598. *Hannibal and Hermes* (lost play), with Drayton and Wilson, all named by Henslowe.

1598. *Pierce of Winchester* (lost play), with Drayton and Wilson, all named by Henslowe.

1598. *Worse Afeard than Hurt* (lost play), with Drayton. Henslowe's entries about this play are confusing, and Greg supposed it to be a second part of *Hannibal and Hermes*. After the first entry on July 28, "in full payment of a boocke called haneball & hermes other wisse called worse feared then hurte," Henslowe never uses the title *Hannibal* again. As he had already paid six pounds for that play, he was really making the *first* payment on *Worse Afeared*.

1598. *The First Civil Wars of France* (lost play), with Drayton, both named by Henslowe.

1598. *Connan Prince of Cornwall* (lost play), with Drayton, both named by Henslowe.

1598. Part II of *The Civil Wars of France* (lost play), with Drayton, both named by Henslowe.

1598. Part III of *The Civil Wars of France* (lost play), with Drayton, both named by Henslowe.

1599. *The First Introduction of the Civil Wars of France* (lost play); Henslowe names Dekker.

1599. *Troilus and Cressida,* with Chettle. Henslowe names both. Only a manuscript fragment of the prompter's plot-outline of this play survives.

1599. *Agamemnon or Orestes Furious* (lost play), with Chettle. Both named by Henslowe.

1599. *The Shoemaker's Holiday.* Henslowe names Dekker only. Published in 1600.

1599. *The Stepmother's Tragedy* (lost play), with Chettle, both named by Henslowe.

1599. *Bear a Brain* (lost play). Henslowe names Dekker.

1599. *The Lamentable Tragedy of Page of Plymouth* (lost play), with Jonson, both named by Henslowe.

1599. *Robert II or The Scot's Tragedy* (lost play), with Jonson, Chettle, and an "other Jentellman," probably Marston. See Foakes, 124.

1599. *Patient Grissill,* with Chettle and Haughton, all named by Henslowe. Henslowe's payments total £10. 10s.; the last two, those of 28 and 29 December, are "earnests" and may represent promises for a second part. Published in 1603.

1599. *The Whole History of Fortunatus.* See the discussion in Chapter 2. Published in 1600.

1600. *Truth's Supplication to Candlelight* (lost play). Henslowe names Dekker. Payments total only forty shillings; the play may not have been finished.

1600. *The Spanish Moor's Tragedy* (lost play), with Day and Haughton, all named by Henslowe. See the comments on *Lust's Dominion,* Part C, below.

1600. *The Seven Wise Masters* (lost play), with Day, Haughton, and Chettle, all named by Henslowe.

1600. *The Golden Ass or Cupid and Psyche* (lost play), with Day and Chettle, all named by Henslowe.

1600. *The Fair Constance of Rome* (lost play), with Drayton, Hathway, Munday, and Wilson, all named by Henslowe.

1600. *Fortune's Tennis* (lost play). Henslowe names Dekker.

1601. *Satiromastix.* The title page names Dekker. Published in 1602.

1601. *Blurt, Master Constable.* With an unknown collaborator? Assigned to Dekker on internal evidence. Published in 1602.

1601. *King Sebastian of Portugal* (lost play), with Chettle, both named by Henslowe.

1602. Prologue and Epilogue to *Pontius Pilate* (lost play). Henslowe names Dekker.

1602. Alterations of *Tasso's Melancholy* (lost play). Henslowe names Dekker. The play was new on August 11, 1594.

1602. *Jeptha* (lost play), with Munday, both named by Henslowe.

1602. *Caesar's Fall, or The Two Shapes* (lost play), with Munday, Drayton, Middleton, and Webster, all named by Henslowe.

1602. *A Medicine for a Curst Wife* (lost play). Henslowe names Dekker.

1602. Additions to *Sir John Oldcastle.* Henslowe names Dekker. If these additions were to Part II, as seems likely, they have been lost.

1602. [*Sir Thomas Wyatt*]. Part I of *Lady Jane* (probably also titled *The Overthrow of Rebels*), with Webster, Chettle, Heywood, and Smith, all named by Henslowe. This and Part II of *Lady Jane* probably survive, much abridged, in *Sir Thomas Wyatt,* published in 1607 as by Dekker and Webster.

1602. [*Sir Thomas Wyatt*]. Part II of *Lady Jane.* Henslowe names Dekker only.

1602. Commendatory verses for Anthony Munday, *The Third and Last Part of Palmerin of England,* signed by Dekker. (The verses may have been written earlier, for the edition of 1602 was not the first of this romance.)

1602. *Christmas Comes But Once a Year* (lost play), with Webster, Chettle, and Heywood, all named by Henslowe.

1603. Commendatory verses for Anthony Munday, *A True and Admirable History of a Maiden of Confolens,* signed by Dekker.

1603. *The Magnificent Entertainment Given to King James,* with Jonson and Middleton. Published in 1604.

1603. *The Wonderful Year.* Published anonymously in late 1603 or early 1604; but Dekker clearly claims the tract in *The Seven Deadly Sins.*

1604. *News from Gravesend.* Anonymous; but see Wilson, xi–xvi.

1604. Commendatory verses for Stephen Harrison, *The Arches of Triumph Erected in Honor of James I,* signed by Dekker.

1604. Part I of *The Honest Whore,* with Middleton, both named by Henslowe.

1604. *Westward Ho!,* with Webster, both named on the title page. Published in 1607.

1605. *Northward Ho!,* with Webster, both named on the title page. Published in 1607.

1605–1607?. Part II of *The Honest Whore.* Entered in the Register on April 29, 1608; published in 1630 with Dekker's name on the title page.

1605. *The Roaring Girl,* with Middleton, both named on the title page. Published in 1611.

1605. *The Double PP.* Anonymous, but assignable to Dekker on internal evidence. See F. P. Wilson, "Dekker, Segar, and Some Others," *Huntington Library Quarterly,* XVIII (1954–1955), 297–300. Published in 1606.

1606. *The Whore of Babylon.* Dekker's name is on the title page. Published in 1607.

1606. *The Seven Deadly Sins of London.* Dekker's name is on the title page.

1606. *News from Hell.* Dekker's name is on the title page.

1607. [*News from Hell* enlarged as] *A Knight's Conjuring.* Dekker's name is on the title page.

1607. *Jests to Make You Merry . . . Unto Which is Added The Misery of a Prison,* with "T. D. and George Wilkins" on the title page and "T. D. and G. W." after the epistle. Part of the manuscript was in Dekker's autograph.

1607. *The Dead Term.* Dekker's name is on the title page. Entered on November 3, 1607; title page dated 1608.

1608. *The Great Frost. Cold Doings in London, Except It Be at the Lottery.* Entered in the Register on February 1, 1608. This tract has been ascribed to Dekker by Arber, Jones-Davies, and Wilson, all independently, and the attribution is probably correct. I have read the tract only in the reprint; see *An English Garner,* ed. by E. Arber, VII (Westminster: A. Constable & Co., 1903) 163–185. See also *The Cold Year,* 1615, below.

1608. *The Bellman of London.* Anonymous; but in the epistle in *Lanthorn and Candlelight,* signed by Dekker, he claims both that work and this.

1608. *Lanthorn and Candlelight.* The epistle is signed by Dekker.

1608. *The Gull's Hornbook.* Dekker's name is on the title page. Published in 1609.

1608. *The Raven's Almanac.* The epistle is signed "T. Deckers." Entered in the Register on July 7, 1608; first edition dated 1609.

1609. *Work for Armorers.* Dekker's name is on the title page.

1609. *Four Birds of Noah's Ark.* The epistle is signed by Dekker.

1611. *If This Be Not a Good Play, the Devil Is in It.* Topical references fit events of late 1610 and early 1611. Published in 1612 with Dekker's name on the title page. See A. Freeman, "The Date of Dekker's *If This Be Not a Good Play, the Devil Is in It,*" *Philological Quarterly,* XLIV (1965), 122–124.

1610? 1611? *The Life and Death of Guy of Warwick,* with Day, both named in the entry in the Register, 1620. Greg says it is uncertain whether this play is identical with *The Tragical History of Guy Earl of Warwick,* which was published in 1661 and has apparently never been reprinted. Bullen and Bentley doubt the identity; see Bentley, V, 1348. I have not seen *The Tragical History.*

1612. [*Lanthorn and Candlelight* enlarged as] *O per se O . . . Being an Addition or Lengthening of the Bellman's Second Night-Walk.* See *Lanthorn and Candlelight,* 1608.

1612. *Troia Nova Triumphans.* Dekker's name is on the title page.

1612. *A Strange Horse-Race.* Dekker's name is on the title page. Published in 1613.

1615. [*The Great Frost* recast as] *The Cold Year 1614.* Mme. Jones-Davies says that "whole paragraphs, too numerous to cite, are borrowed from *The Great Frost*," 1608, and that the pamphlet has other traits of Dekker's hand, II, 383.

1615. Commendatory verses for John Taylor, *Taylor's Urania or His Heavenly Muse*, signed by Dekker.

1615. *The Artillery Garden*. Entered in the Register on November 29, with Dekker's name. A quarto edition published in 1616 seems to have disappeared excepting one copy discovered by F. P. Wilson in 1936.

1616. [*O per se O* reissued as] *Villainies Discovered...O per se O...Newly Corrected and Enlarged. Villainies* contains seven chapters on prisons and prisoners. (See *Lanthorn and Candlelight*, 1608.)

1616. Six "Prison Characters" added to the Overbury *Characters*, ninth edition. See W. J. Paylor, *The Overburian Characters* (Oxford: B. Blackwell, 1936), "Introduction," xxv–xxxi, for a description.

1617. *Certain Characters and Essays of Prison and Prisoners*, with Geoffrey Mynshull. Dekker's work is clearly evident in the last fourth of the book, three essays and three characters. In the earlier portions the Euphuistic style shows Mynshull's participation. See Philip Shaw, "Dekker's Position in Prison Literature," *PMLA*, LXII (1947), 386–388. Published in 1618.

1619. *Dekker's Dream*. Entered on October 11, 1619; title page dated 1620.

1620–1624? *The Telltale*. Survives as an anonymous manuscript play, printed by the Malone Society, 1960. See Arthur Freeman,

"The Authorship of *The Tell-Tale*," *Journal of English and Germanic Philology*, LXII (1963), 288–292. This play is surely Dekker's.

1620–1623? *Match Me in London*. Dekker's name is on the title page. Published in 1631.

1620. *The Virgin Martyr*, with Massinger. Published in 1622 with both authors' names on the title page.

1621. *The Witch of Edmonton*, with Rowley, Ford, "&c." Published in 1658. The "&c." is probably the publisher's guess and is disregarded by most scholars.

1622? *The Noble Spanish Soldier*, with Day. Dekker is named in Sir Henry Herbert's license.

1623. *The Bellman of Paris* (lost play), with Day, both named by Herbert in the license of July 30.

1623? *The Wonder of a Kingdom* (with Day, if this play is the same as *Come See a Wonder*, licensed by Herbert on 18 September as by Day alone). Twice entered in the Register as by Dekker alone and with his name only on the title page of the first edition, 1636. Borrowings from Day's *The Parliament of Bees* are extensive.

1624. *The Sun's Darling*, with Ford, both named in Herbert's license and on the title page. Published in 1656.

1624. *The Fairy Knight* (lost play), with Ford, both named in Herbert's license.

1624. *The Late Murder in Whitechapel, or Keep the Widow Waking* (lost play), with Ford, Rowley, and Webster, all named in legal documents. See Bentley, III, 252–256, for a summary of the case.

1624. *The Bristow Merchant* (lost play), with Ford, both named in Herbert's license. *Penny-Wise, Pound-Foolish,* 1630, also tells of a merchant of Bristol.

1624? *The Welsh Embassador,* a recasting of *The Noble Spanish Soldier* (1622?) into comedy, possibly with Ford; but only Dekker's name is given for this play in Hill's list of manuscripts in the late seventeenth century. See Bowers, IV, 303.

1625. *A Rod for Runaways.* Dekker's name is on the title page and ends the epistle.

1626. *The Tale of Joconda and Astolso* (lost play). Dekker is named as author in the Register, June 29, 1660. Bentley conjectures a date of composition about 1630–1632, III, 265.

1627. Lord Mayor's show for the inauguration of Sir Hugh Hamersley. Lost, but mentioned by Dekker in the epistle of *Wars, Wars, Wars,* 1628, sigs. A$_2$v, A$_3$. See also "Of unknown date," below, after 1632.

1628. *Look Up and See Wonders.* "Has all the characteristics of Dekker's style," says Wilson, p. xxiii.

1628. *Wars, Wars, Wars.* Dekker signs the epistle.

1628. *Brittannia's Honor.* Dekker's name is on the title page.

1629. *London's Tempe.* Dekker's name is on the title page.

1630. *London, Look Back.* Ascribed by Wilson on internal evidence.

1630. *The Black Rod and the White Rod.* Ascribed by Wilson on internal evidence.

1630. *Penny-Wise, Pound-Foolish.* Dekker is named in the entry in the Register, December 17. Published in 1631.

1631? *Gustavus King of Swethland* (lost play). Cited as Dekker's in Aaron Hill's list of manuscript plays, late in the seventeenth century. Joseph Quincy Adams, "Hill's List of Early Plays in Manuscript," *The Library,* 4th series, XX (1939–1940), 71–99.

1632. Commendatory verses for Richard Brome, *The Northern Lass,* signed by Dekker.

1632. "Paul his temple triumphant," manuscript poem on the repairing of St. Paul's Cathedral; epistle signed "Tho: Dekker." Printed by F. David Hoeniger, *Renaissance News,* XVI (1963), 194–200.

Of unknown date:

Believe It Is So and 'Tis So (lost play), cited as Dekker's in Hill's list of manuscript plays. Identified by Professor Harbage with *Perkin Warbeck;* see II, "Secondary Sources."

A City Show on the Lord Mayor's Day (possibly *Britannia's Honor* or *London's Tempe;* see also 1627, above); cited as Dekker's in Hill's list.

Disguises, Love in Disguise, a Petticoat Voyage (all one play, lost), cited as Dekker's in Hill's list. Possibly this is the play called by Henslowe *The Disguises,* and for which he records his share of the box office in October and November, 1595. He does not name the author. Foakes and Rickert, pp. 31–33.

The White Moor (lost play?), cited as Dekker's in Hill's list. Bentley rejects the supposition that Dekker's play survives as *The White Ethiopian,* a manuscript play in the British Museum, III, 269.

B. WORKS WRONGLY ASCRIBED TO DEKKER

Scholars of varying degrees of authority, and with varying degrees of confidence, have attributed the following works to Thomas Dekker. Not one of the items, however, has been assigned to him with anything like unanimity. In rejecting them, therefore, and other conjectures less worthy of mention, I am not opposing any settled tradition. To explain fully the bases for rejection of each would require too much space; I make only a brief comment. I list the works alphabetically.

The Bachelor's Banquet (1603). To the cogent reasons which Wilson offers for denying the attribution may be added the absence of allusions to London life which Dekker would inevitably have used. F. P. Wilson, ed., "Introduction," *The Batchelars Banquet* (Oxford: Clarendon Press, 1929).

The Bloody Banquet (published 1639). Bentley and Schoenbaum see no real evidence of Dekker's authorship. Nothing in the style or dramaturgy recalls Dekker's work. Samuel Schoenbaum, ed., *The Bloody Banquet* (The Malone Society: Oxford University Press, 1962), p. vi.

Canaan's Calamity (1598; published in 1618). In style this is too pedestrian and unimaginative for Dekker in 1598. The spelling and other accidentals do not indicate a manuscript by him. Even Miss Hunt, who accepts the attribution, complains of the flat style. Mann believes Deloney is the author. F. O. Mann, ed., *The Works of Thomas Deloney* (Oxford: Clarendon Press, 1912), pp. 593–594.

Captain Thomas Stukeley. Henslowe does not name the author (1596). Published without ascription in 1605. Judging by the style, this play may be in part by Heywood.

Chance Medley (1598). Chambers, III, 302, says Henslowe paid Dekker "or Chettle" for this play, now lost. A better reading of the *Diary,* however, shows that Henslowe erred in regard to the authors, who were Robert Wilson, Henry Chettle, Michael Drayton, and Anthony Munday. See Foakes and Rickert, pp. 96–97.

[William Fennor]. *The Counter's Commonwealth* (1616; published in 1617). I cannot agree with Shaw that Dekker contributed to this prison tract. Philip Shaw, "Dekker's Position in Prison Literature," *PMLA,* LXII (1947), 382–385. Dekker may have borrowed from Fennor, who writes from the Counter prison, whereas Dekker was in King's Bench.

The Additions to *Doctor Faustus,* 1602. Greg does not believe that Dekker's style or handiwork can be detected in the additions; I agree. W. W. Greg, *Marlowe's Doctor Faustus 1604–1616* (Oxford: Oxford University Press, 1950), p. 135.

The Fairy Knight, or Oberon the Second. This manuscript play, which I have not seen, is probably not related to Dekker's and Ford's collaboration of 1624 (*The Fairy Knight*), says Bentley, III, 250.

The Family of Love (registered in 1607, published in 1608). After several attempts to discover evidence for either Dekker or Middleton (to whom this play is usually assigned), I conclude that it belongs to neither of them.

Grievous Groans for the Poor (registered on January 16, 1621). Certainly not by Dekker.

The London Prodigal (published in 1605). Among the more important reasons why this domestic drama should not be assigned to Dekker are these: the sketchy use of Dutch dialect only for disguise, not for humor (whereas the Southwestern dialect is elaborated with great care for humor), and some most uncharacteristic omissions—of the comic servant or clown, of speaking in chorus, of flashes of poetry and eloquence, of all traces of Dekker's spelling, and of his usual figures and diction.

Lust's Dominion (published in 1657). Scholarly opinion has been equally divided for and against Dekker's participation in the making of *Lust's Dominion*. No doubt editors should be granted more authority than other scholars in deciding on authenticity; and two editors, Brereton and Bowers, attribute the play at least partly to Dekker. But Professor Bowers makes no defense for including *Lust's Dominion* in the canon except for its conjectural identity with *The Spanish Moor's Tragedy*, 1600, a work which Henslowe mentions but once, after paying Dekker, Day, and Haughton only three pounds "in parte of payment." It is only a conjecture that that play was ever finished. Really, then, we are left to deal with *Lust's Dominion* on internal evidence, which Brereton believed he found, though it was almost wholly in the diction, "parallel passages." Professor Bowes says nothing of Dekker's spelling being discernible in the play, and in fact finds the scene division quite different from Dekker's practice (V, 127). It seems to me that Dekker's responsibility for this play remains very doubtful.

The Meeting of Gallants at an Ordinary (1604). Wilson includes this in his edition of Dekker's *Plague Pamphlets*. But he is much too complimentary to the literary merits of the tract, which are weak at best; and he ends his introduction to *Gallants* less confidently than he begins it. The verse is too rough and shapeless for either Dekker or Middleton; the anecdotes are tedious; and there is no raciness in the style or pathos or poignancy in the content. Dekker's spellings do not appear.

The Merry Devil of Edmonton (published in 1608). Only a mangled text of this play survives; but nothing in its style or substance as comedy definitely argues for Dekker's composition. Abrams's list of parallels is a feeble one. W. A. Abrams, ed., *The Merry Devil of Edmonton* (Durham: Duke University Press, 1942), pp. 72–103. A weaker dramatist like Haughton or Wilson is a more likely candidate for the authorship.

The Owl's Almanac (published 1618). Professor Don Cameron Allen, in his edition of this tract (Baltimore: Johns Hopkins Press, 1943), p. 6, rejects the

Selected Bibliography

attribution of this satire to Dekker, but one would like stronger reasons than those he offers. It is a poorer imitation of Nashe than Dekker is capable of, more doggedly jocose, more methodical in satire, less whimsical. Even long imprisonment could scarcely have worked as much change in Dekker's manner, compared to *A Knight's Conjuring.*

The Chronicle History of Perkin Warbeck (published in 1634). Professor Harbage has argued that Dekker and Ford collaborated on this play for Queen Henrietta's Men at the Phoenix theater in 1625. Alfred Harbage, "The Mystery of *Perkin Warbeck,*" *Studies in the English Renaissance Drama,* ed. Josephine W. Bennett, Oscar Cargill, and Vernon Hall junior (New York: New York University Press, 1959), pp. 125–141. While believing that Dekker's craftsmanship deserves the praise that Professor Harbage gives it, I still can find nothing but Ford's diction, character-drawing, poetry, and themes in the play; I see nothing of Dekker.

The Weakest Goeth to the Wall (published in 1600). The character of the botcher, Barnaby Bunch, has an obvious resemblance to Dekker's servant-clowns; but Dekker did not invent the type or monopolize it, and Miss Hunt makes too much of the resemblance, which is not supported by other evidence of Dekker's revision of a play by Chettle. Whoever the author was, he seems to have prepared the manuscript with care for the press.

C. SOME CONJECTURAL REVISIONS

Below is a list of early plays which Fleay and others have conjectured may originally have been composed by Dekker and then revised by him and his collaborators during Jacobean or Caroline times. Most of the originals are mentioned by Henslowe. Undoubtedly *The Noble Spanish Soldier* (a Jacobean, not an Elizabethan play) was revised into *The Welsh Embassador;* but I know of no proof that such full-scale revision was given any other of Dekker's surviving plays, and it is hard to instance other examples of such rewriting in English Renaissance drama. All the plays in this list have apparently been lost in their original form. The chronological order brings the items into relation with those in the "Authentic Works" above.

More detail about these speculations will be found in Chambers, III, "Thomas Dekker."

1594. *Philipo and Hippolito,* revised as *Philenzo and Hypollita,* which was entered in the Register in 1660 as by Massinger. Both are lost. Dekker's connection with *Philipo* is a weak inference.

1594. *The Set at Maw,* as *Match Me in London* (1620-23?).

1594. *Diocletian* (Chambers erroneously gives 1599), as *The Virgin Martyr* (1620).

1594. *The Venetian Comedy,* as *The Jew of Venice.* See the first item in "Authentic Works" above.

1594. *The French Doctor,* as *The Jew of Venice.* See the first item "Authentic Works," above.

? *Antony and Valia* (revived in 1595), as *Antonio and Vallia,* entered in the Register in 1660 as by Massinger.

1595. *The Mack,* as *The Wonder of a Kingdom* (1623?).
1595. *The Disguises,* as *Disguises, or Love in Disguise, a Petticoat Voyage* in Hill's list (see the end of "Authentic Works" above).
1600. *Truth's Supplication to Candlelight,* as *The Whore of Babylon* (1606). A most unlikely identification.
1602. *The Spanish Fig,* as *The Noble Spanish Soldier* (1622?).
1610? 1611? *The Life and Death of Guy of Warwick,* as *The Tragical History of Guy Earl of Warwick* (published in 1661). See "Authentic Works" above.

II. SECONDARY SOURCES

Bibliographies that were intended to be exhaustive of criticism and scholarship on Dekker are included in the *Cambridge Bibliography of English Literature,* edited by F. W. Bateson, II (Cambridge: Cambridge University Press, 1941); in its *Supplement: A. D. 600–1900,* edited by George Watson (Cambridge: Cambridge University Press, 1957); and in S. A. Tannenbaum, *Thomas Dekker: A Concise Bibliography* New York: S. A. Tannenbaum, 1939). Because of the availability of these works, as well as of annual bibliographies of Renaissance literature, the following list is highly selective. It is meant to include the more notable critical and scholarly books and articles down to 1966, exclusive of those already cited in preceding chapters and notes. The importance of many of the cited works has been made clear at least by implication. For economy of space all doctoral dissertations are omitted.

In passing it is worth observing that the study of Dekker during the twentieth century has been advanced by the work of a remarkable number of eminent bibliographers and textual scholars, including Fredson Bowers, F. P. Wilson, R. B. McKerrow, James G. McManaway, Sir Walter Greg, and others. Some of their contributions have been mentioned in the text; a few others are listed below.

Adkins, M. G. M. "Puritanism in the Plays and Pamphlets of Dekker," *University of Texas Studies in English,* XIX (1939), 86-113. Useful more because it reveals the minor touches of satire than because it demonstrates Dekker's actual sympathy with Puritanism.

Bradbrook, Muriel C. *The Growth and Structure of Elizabethan Comedy.* London: Chatto and Windus, 1955. Severely and rather indiscriminately unfavorable criticism. The judgments are very dubious: Dekker is "something of a moral sloven" (125); his pamphlets are "incomparably superior" to his plays (129)!

Brereton, J. Le Gay. "Introduction," *Lust's Dominion; or, The Lascivious Queen. Materials for the Study of the Old English Drama.* Vol. V. Louvain: Ch. Uystpruyst, 1931. Good accounts of Dekker's characterization and style. The most convincing argument for Dekker's authorship of this play.

Brown, Arthur. "Citizen Comedy and Domestic Drama" in *Jacobean Theatre* (Stratford-Upon-Avon Studies 1). New York: St. Martin's Press, 1960. More restrained than Miss Bradbrook's this critique sums up essentially to the idea that Dekker was a successful entertainer.

Selected Bibliography

Bush, Douglas. *English Literature in the Earlier Seventeenth Century, 1600–1660.* Oxford: Oxford University Press, 1945. Chapter II has the best, brief evaluation of Dekker's non-dramatic work to be found.

Chandler, Frank W. *The Literature of Roguery.* 2 vols. New York: Burt Franklin, 1958 (original publication, 1907). First thorough, though not complete, investigation of Dekker's debt to earlier tracts on cozening and the like.

Cross, K. Gustav. "The Authorship of *Lust's Dominion,*" *Studies in Philology,* LV (1958), 39–61. Believes the extant play to be a revision by Dekker, Haughton, and Marston of an older play; accepts the identification of *Lust's Dominion* with *The Spanish Moor's Tragedy.*

Dodson, Daniel B. "Blurt, Master Constable," *Notes and Queries,* new series, VI (1959), 61–65. Good demonstration of the evidence against Middleton's authorship, but less impressive as a claim for Dekker's.

———. "Allusions to the Gunpowder Plot in Dekker's *The Whore of Babylon,*" *Notes and Queries,* new series, VI (1959), 257. Helps confirm date and inspiration of this play.

Evans, G. Blakemore. "Dryden's *MacFlecknoe* and Dekker's *Satiromastix,*" *Modern Language Notes,* LXXVI (1961), 598–600. Dryden borrows a satiric idea from Dekker and approximates Dekker's attitude toward Jonson, not Shadwell's.

Freeman, Arthur. "The Authorship of *The Tell-Tale,*" *Journal of English and Germanic Philol-* ogy, LXII (1963), 288–292. Goes far toward establishing the play in the Dekker canon. See "Primary Sources" above for 1620.

Halstead, W. L. "Collaboration in *The Patient Grissill,*" *Philological Quarterly,* XVIII (1939), 381–394. Distinguishes the dramatists' shares; to be compared with Greene's article, cited in Chapter III, note 5.

Hazlitt, William. *Lectures on the Dramatic Literature of the Age of Elizabeth* in *The Complete Works of William Hazlitt,* ed. by P. P. Howe, vol. VI. London and Toronto: J. M. Dent and Sons, 1931, pp. 234–240. Fine specimen of Romantic appreciation of character-drawing in Elizabethan drama to the exclusion of almost all other elements. Highly readable.,

Knights, L. C. *Drama and Society in the Age of Jonson.* London: Chatto & Windus, 1937. Somewhat superficial in his harsh strictures on Dekker's dramatic ineptitude, Knights is better on the writer's "citizen morality" and concludes with rather high praise. But in saying that "One cannot classify this morality as either 'medieval' or 'modern,'" Knights leaves us with an unresolved difficulty.

Lange, Alexis F. "Introduction," *The Shoemaker's Holiday* in *Representative English Comedies.* Ed. by C. M. Gayley. Vol. III. New York: Macmillan, 1914. Useful, scholarly appreciation, though written more from the point of view of the student than of the theater audience.

McKerrow, R. B. "Introduction" and "Notes." *The Gull's Hornbook.* London: De la More Press, 1904.

Prepared with McKerrow's usual thoroughness, except as regards collation of all extant copies.

Moore, John R. "The Songs of the Public Theatres in the Time of Shakespeare," *Journal of English and Germanic Philology*, XXVIII (1929), 166–202. Good survey of the use of song in popular drama. Dekker is treated *passim*.

Murray, Peter B. "The Collaboration of Dekker and Webster in *Northward Ho* and *Westward Ho*," *Papers of the Bibliographical Society of America*, LVI (1962) 482–486. Application of contemporary bibliographical methods to discovery of contributions and methods of collaboration.

Novarr, David. "Dekker's Gentle Craft and the Lord Mayor of London," *Modern Philology*, LVII (1959–1960), 233–239. Dekker seems to have utilized a recent Lord Mayor's vain effort to prevent the love-match of his daughter.

Peery, William. "*The Noble Soldier* and *The Parliament of Bees*," *Studies in Philology*, XLVIII (1951), 219–233. A good introduction to the problematical relations of these plays and to previous investigations of them. But Peery dates *Parliament of Bees* later than the evidence warrants. Day himself probably borrowed from it for *Noble Soldier*.

Pierce, Frederick E. *The Collaboration of Webster and Dekker*. New York: Henry Holt, 1909. Most comprehensive attempt yet made to discriminate the shares of the dramatists. Chief basis of F. L. Lucas's conclusions in his edition of Webster.

Power, William. "Double, Double," *Notes and Queries*, CCIV (1959), 4–8. Intending to claim the portrait of Moll Frith in *The Roaring Girl* for Middleton, this article also makes some useful comments on Dekker.

Price, George R. "The Shares of Middleton and Dekker in a Collaborated Play," *Papers of the Michigan Academy of Science, Arts and Letters*, XXX (1945), 601–615. Analysis of *The Roaring Girl*, chiefly on the basis of style.

Reynolds, George F. "The Aims of a Popular Elizabethan Dramatist," *Philological Quarterly*, XX (1941), 340–344. Prologue to *If This Be Not a Good Play* considered as expressive of Dekker's esthetic purposes.

Routh, Harold V. "London and the Development of Popular Literature," *Cambridge History of English Literature*. Vol. IV. New York: G. P. Putnam's Sons, 1910. Sound discussion well worth reading.

Sharpe, Robert B. *The Real War of the Theaters*. Boston: D. C. Heath, 1935. Enlightening survey of the London theatrical world in which Dekker grew to maturity (1594–1604).

Toliver, Harold E. "*The Shoemaker's Holiday:* Theme and Image," *Boston University Studies in English*, V (1961), 208–218. Attempts to reveal a greater depth of significance than has generally been found in the play.

Index

Index

[*185*]

Index

Index